QUESTION TIME

QUESTION TIME

?

DAVID COOK

ivp
Inter-Varsity Press

INTER-VARSITY PRESS
38 De Montfort Street, Leicester LE1 7GP, England
Email: ivp@uccf.org.uk Website: www.ivpbooks.com

First published 2002

British Library Cataloguing in Publication Data
A catalogue record for this book is available from the British Library.

ISBN 0–85111–482–2

Set in Adobe Garamond 11/13pt
Typeset in Great Britain by CRB Associates, Reepham, Norfolk
Printed and bound in Great Britain by Creative Print and Design (Wales), Ebbw Vale

Inter-Varsity Press is the publishing division of the Universities and Colleges Christian Fellowship (formerly the Inter-Varsity Fellowship), a student movement linking Christian Unions in universities and colleges throughout Great Britain, and a member movement of the International Fellowship of Evangelical Students. For more information about local and national activities write to UCCF, 38 De Montfort Street, Leicester LE1 7GP, email us at email@uccf.org.uk, or visit the UCCF website at www.uccf.org.uk.

Dedication

To Oliver Barclay in gratitude for his vision for and enabling of the Whitefield Institute.

His concern is always that Christian teaching be lived out in practice.

Contents

General introduction

'What right do you have to tell anyone else what to do?' 'What right do you have to inflict your morality on other people?' These are two of the most common responses to Christians whenever they make some comment on a personal or social moral issue. It is almost as if Christians are not allowed to hold any moral views at all, far less to express them publicly. Sadly, it seems in our secular, post-modern society that holding any kind of moral view or deep conviction is tantamount to being an extremist.

My response to such questions is simple and direct. I do not have any right to tell anyone else what to do. When I express Christian views, I am really trying to state God's view rather than my own opinion. I believe that God has revealed his standards and his way in the Bible and in the life and teaching of Jesus Christ. God's standards judge me and all human beings. They are his rules and guidelines for human behaviour and how we should live. If I am honest, there are times when I would like these rules to be different and far easier. All too often I fall short of the standard that God expects. But that does not change the fact that God has standards and that we are answerable to the creator God for the way we live and the choices we make.

I have absolutely no right to inflict my morality on other people. We live, however, in a democratic, free society, where I am as entitled to express my views as anyone and everyone else. I do not want to inflict anything on anyone, but I do want to give people an opportunity to understand another perspective and to help them think very carefully about the moral issues of the day, their personal outlook and beliefs and what perspectives Christianity has to offer. As a Christian, I have a responsibility to share God's good news with others. Part of what it means to be a Christian is to try to be like salt and light in society. That inevitably must mean tossing Christian perspectives into the maelstrom of today's moral confusion.

Each week, Radio 4's 'The Moral Maze' (the unkind call it the Moral Zoo) explores a current moral issue taken from the week's news. A series of witnesses are cross-examined and the panel respond in a robust, even at times rude, manner. The panel does not represent anyone but themselves. Of course, each panellist has a general line he or she usually takes, though there are surprising variations. Over a million people listen to the programme, and in its way it has become a minor national institution. In the complexity and variety of moral issues facing all of us as individuals and as a society, we are not just deeply interested and fascinated by moral topics, we are desperate for some help.

Business people, doctors and nurses, social workers, teachers and all professional groups are enthusiastic to have input in helping think through appropriate responses to moral questions. Usually, such people do not want to be told what to do, certainly not in any authoritarian, closed way. They do want to be guided, directed and encouraged to work things out for themselves.

When it comes to personal problems, the same need for input and insight is clearly there. Counsellors of every variety will testify to the growth of a 'listening' and 'advising' industry. Indeed, most clergy and ministers no longer see visiting as simply pastoral care but as giving time and space to help people cope with difficult personal, family and social problems.

Our society no longer seems well equipped to face the moral issues of the day. We are, however, still deeply concerned about the environment, our families, sexual behaviour and attitudes, justice, poverty, force and violence, racism, sexism, social welfare and the hosts of particular problems thrown up by technology, politics, medicine, business and life in general in the twenty-first century.

When travelling, there are times when you are happy to chat and times when you just want to be left alone. If I want to kill conversation stone dead, I wait for the 'What do you do for a living?' question. 'I teach philosophy' is a cast iron guarantee of silence. If I say, however, that I teach ethics or medical ethics, that produces a stream of problems, opinions, questions and debate which guarantees lengthy discussion. In pubs, clubs, public meetings, professional gatherings and all sorts of social settings people are concerned about moral issues. They have deeply held views and they delight to propound and debate them. They have strong feelings and emotional reactions about moral issues.

This book is meant to help Christians, in particular, to think more biblically about moral issues. It is also meant to help those who have no Christian perspective to understand how Christians are working out their faith and trying to apply it to the moral questions facing all of us. I have tried to avoid over-simplistic answers because they are few and far between and often do more harm than good. The responses to each of the questions explored does not pretend to offer the last word in Christian ethical reflection. Rather, it offers what in the television programme 'University Challenge' is called a 'starter for ten'. It is meant to provide a way in to exploring the moral questions and a means of beginning to apply biblical perspectives. The validity and worth of the Christian moral view is assumed. This is not the place to produce a defence for that, but instead to focus on what it means in practice.

The book will be worthwhile if it helps people to understand Christian perspectives on moral issues and to think through not just the issues specifically dealt with here, but also the moral problems yet to come. In my teaching of Christian ethics, the aim is not so much to give answers to today's problems, but rather to ensure that, no matter what new questions may arise in the future, people will be able to start from first principles and produce genuine Christian answers.

No book is produced without a great deal of practical help and encouragement. Colin Duriez and IVP have been patient, faithful and consistent in their commitment to seeing this book in print. Grant Vallance, Katie Wasson, Lee Wells and Candy Claridge did much of the research and information collection. Nyla Spawn did the initial typing, and Ruth Robinson, in particular, did a splendid job of typing and editing the manuscript.

The format of the book is simple and consistent. Each topic is set out by looking at the background of why this is a problem and what issues are at stake. Then society's responses, how people today are thinking and feeling about each issue, are explored and outlined. Then Christian perspectives are expressed, looking at the principles, the consequences and what it means to put Christian morality into practice. The Bible is concerned about the principles of what God declares to be right, wrong, good and bad. It is also concerned about the consequences of what we say and do and how we live. There are effects in the here and now as well as in eternity. The Bible's main concern, however, is how we should live as the people of God. We are to be salt and light, living copies of Christ. We are to incarnate the teaching and example of Jesus. Christian ethics is a way of living.

1
Social fashion

A dedicated follower of fashion

We are social animals. We need and enjoy company, but we can behave differently when we are in a crowd. It is all too easy just to go along with what everyone else is doing. Kierkegaard said that the crowd is a lie. He was suggesting that we do things as part of a crowd that we would never do if we were on our own or really thought about what we were doing, why we were doing it and the consequences of our actions. Christians need to consider very carefully the impact of others on what we think and do. Our behaviour can easily be shaped by the world and people around us. We need to ask when it is good and right to behave just the same as other people and when it is important to behave differently. This might be because we know some things to be right and others wrong and that we realize the consequences of our actions and lifestyles. This section examines some of the questions people ask about their behaviour in social settings.

How far should I follow fashion?

Background to the problem

If we walk down any city street in the evening, we will meet crowds of young people all decked out in the latest fashion. If we buy any magazine, the pages are full of the fashionable places, people, style and things to do. Fashion magazines are full of models who look like stick insects or macho men with a touch of the caring soul. Advertising depends on what is in fashion and changes in fashion, whether this is in terms of music, television programmes, clothes, consumer goods or body image. It seems as if we are what we buy – *tesco ergo sum*, 'I shop therefore I am'. We are all subject to peer group pressure and the desire to conform.

This is not just about personal or social taste. It is also about money and the millions of pounds that are spent each day on buying and selling what is in fashion. What does this desire to follow fashion tell us about ourselves, and what moral choices does it create for us?

Society's responses

In theory, we are all unique individuals living in a world where no-one has the right to tell us what to do. Yet the pattern of advertising and the success of selling and buying shows that we actually want to conform to the latest in what is considered good taste and the height of fashion.

We like to be thought of as fashionable. It gives us a sense of belonging. It makes us fit in with the 'in' crowd. It shows that we are modern and up-to-date with the latest fad. It also reveals the level of our success and affluence. We can afford to keep up with fashion and its changes, even if we have to go into debt to do so. In some parts of traditional Africa the fashion was for powerful men to have a number of large wives. Both the number and size of the wives showed the affluence and wealth of the man by his ability to support and feed these women. Power in the West is shown by lifestyle, fashion and the gadgets we own. Of course, we are not slaves to fashion. We make free choices, which just happen to lead us to make similar choices to what is in fashion.

In a post-modern society there will be those who dare to be different, yet fashion has remarkable power over us. Society recognizes that the young and the vulnerable, in particular, need to be protected from unfair and inappropriate advertising and pressure. So there is control over advertising. The restrictions on the content, timing and placing of cigarette adverts show that society does wish to safeguard not just the vulnerable but everyone who might be affected. The withdrawal of certain Benetton adverts showed that there are images society refuses to use to sell products. Nevertheless, in light of the health hazards of smoking, the fact that there is any cigarette advertising at all shows the power of advertising, money and the importance of the free choice of the individual.

Christian perspectives

'Don't let the world squeeze you into its mould' is Paul's advice (Romans 12:2 JBP). He warned against the danger of blind, unthinking conformity. It is vital that Christians do not reject the good things that God has provided for us and the things made by human beings expressing the creative power which is the gift of God. But there is always a danger of becoming slaves to fashion, materialism and to those around us. What we treasure reveals where our heart is (Matthew 6:21).

There is no reason for Christians to be old fashioned and dowdy and dress like 'granolas'. We need to be discriminating people who make right and good judgments about what is worth having and following and what needs to be rejected or handled with care. Part of what it means to be a good steward of all that God has given is to ask ourselves whether there is a good reason for having this item of clothing or fashion accessory. All the time there is the danger of materialism and the kind of worry that comes with our concern to have things as well as the risk that we may be drawn into a world of possessions where things matter more than people and appearance more than reality (1 John 2:15–17).

The risk in going along with the crowd is that we will end up in places and doing things that we would be far better to avoid. In the book of Proverbs there is a picture of womanhood where the worthy woman is clothed not only in fine linen and purple but, even more importantly, in strength and dignity (Proverbs 31:22, 25). This thought is echoed by Paul in his command to 'Clothe yourselves with the Lord Jesus Christ' (Romans 13:14). The inner reality is more important than the outward show, but to be real it must show itself in how we live.

It is interesting that Jesus was often attacked because he seemed to be one of the crowd and spent his time eating and drinking with 'bad company'. Yet it is crystal clear that Jesus challenged the fashions of his day whether secular or religious. We must have his discriminating power.

Something to think about

Is what I want good or bad, wholesome or unwholesome?
Why do I want to wear the clothes I do?
Am I simply being pressurized by others?
Do I own and control? Or am I owned and controlled?
What limits do I draw? Why?

What is wrong with smoking and drinking?

Background to the problem

In any social gathering, you will see and smell people smoking and drinking. Recently there has been a dramatic attempt to create no-smoking settings and also campaigns to encourage people not to drink and drive. Alcohol and tobacco have long been used for relaxation and enjoyment. There has been tremendous pressure in social contexts to conform and to join in with smoking and drinking. However, there is a growing awareness of the damage that smoking does, not only to the smoker but also to others, including both the child in the womb and any of us who are affected by so-called 'passive' smoking. Awareness of the addictive quality of alcohol and tobacco, the terrible effects of smoking and drinking on the health of people, and the sexual, physical and verbal abuse, as well as dangerous driving, which result from drunkenness, has created questions for society about what controls should be introduced. How far should we be allowed to use substances that harm us and can lead to harm and costs to others? This is a hard question for governments, who derive vast income from the tax on alcohol and smoking products, yet are also financially liable for the massive health-care costs resulting from smoking and alcohol-related diseases.

Society's responses

It is quite clear that smoking and drinking patterns, both within and between nations, vary from total abstinence to abuse. Smoking and drinking are cultural and social activities and differ from culture to culture. People hold very dear the freedom of individuals to do whatever they want with their own bodies and money. There is a fear of the 'Nanny' state and unwanted restrictions. Yet there is deep concern about the dangers of smoking and drinking and their impact on people. There is overwhelming evidence that smoking is harmful both to the smoker and those in close proximity. The evidence in relation to alcohol is more confusing. There are good grounds to indicate that moderate consumption of red wine can have positive health benefits. It is also clear that alcohol is highly addictive and can very easily lead to abuse and harm to the individual and to others. Dangerous driving, sexual abuse and physical violence often result from alcohol abuse. There is also a loosening of restraint from alcohol use, ranging from relaxation to states of inebriation. This loosening of restraint can lead to lax sexual behaviour and doing things that people regret in the cold light of day.

The role of the law and government varies between health campaigns, explicit warnings on smoking and alcohol products, restrictions on the timing, placing and content of advertising and the regular increasing of tax levels on such products. There is a clear financial embarrassment for politicians because there is a high level of income generated by so called 'sin' taxation, and yet there is an enormous cost in terms of health-care expenditure. The unfortunate effects of an attempt at a total ban in the case of Prohibition in the United States were a dramatic increase in illegal activity and widespread abuse of the law, especially by the wealthy.

Christian perspectives

The Bible doesn't mention smoking, though it does have something to say about alcohol. The psalmist talks of 'wine that gladdens the heart' (Psalm 104:15), and Jesus not only turned water into wine at a wedding in Cana (John 2:1–10) but was constantly accused of spending time in the company of sinners, whose lifestyle was often associated with wine and easy living (Matthew 9:11; 11:19; Mark 2:16; Luke 7:34; 15:1–2).

In New Testament times, water was not particularly safe to drink and so wine was often used to purify the water as well as to improve its taste. Paul urged Timothy to take a little wine for the sake of his stomach and health (1 Timothy 5:23). Wine itself was usually taken in a diluted form, for the dangers of alcohol were all too well known. The prophet Isaiah very vividly warns of the loss of control, the reeling and staggering, the confusion and even vomiting which can follow alcohol abuse (Isaiah 5:11; 28:7–8), and Aaron and his sons were warned of the effects of strong drink and the need for abstinence (Leviticus 10:8–9). The most explicit warnings are embodied in the story of the drunken shame of Noah (Genesis 9:21–23).

In both Galatians and 1 Corinthians, Paul is at pains to stress the freedom that Christians enjoy in Christ. We are no longer bound by systems of rules and legislation and are to avoid legalism, which kills true humanity. But freedom can all too easily become licence. All things may be permissible, but not all things are good for people. The primary responsibility of each of us is to God, to our conscience and to our brother and sister in Christ. Paul argues in Romans 14 that we are not to cause 'weaker' Christians to stumble. We are to recognize the impact of our example and our responsibility for each other in what we do and say. 'It is better not to eat meat or drink wine or to do anything else that will cause your brother to fall' (Romans 14:21).

Christians are also to avoid anything that harms themselves and others. If our bodies are indeed temples of the Holy Spirit (1 Corinthians 3:16), then what we put in them and what we do to and with them is important.

The Christian's concern, however, is not only a principle of proper care of self and prevention of harm, abuse and anything that might lead to addiction. As Christians we need to consider the example and witness given by our behaviour and the lifestyle choices we make. Whether we like it or not, Christianity is judged by the example of Christians. This is why the biblical stress is on being holy, set apart for God, and accordingly different in our outlook and behaviour.

The New Testament urges the followers of Jesus not to be drunk with wine, but rather filled with the Holy Spirit (Ephesians 5:18). In describing the characteristics required of those holding office in the early church, Paul tells Timothy that deacons are not to be 'indulging in much wine' (1 Timothy 3:8).

None of these texts offer an absolute ban on alcohol or smoking. Rather, they point clearly to the dangers and likely consequences of any form of bodily abuse and the need to consider very carefully the impact of our example on others, whether Christian or non-Christian.

Something to think about

Why do I want to smoke or drink?
Am I able to act in moderation?
Have I considered the effects on myself and others?
Can I say 'No'?

Is it OK to use 'harmless' drugs?

Background to the problem

Medicine depends on the proper use of drugs to bring much needed relief from physical and psychological pain and distress. The range of drugs is extensive from the so-called 'hard' drugs like heroin to 'soft' drugs like caffeine in tea and coffee. What can be used for good and human benefit can all too easily lead to abuse, dependency and negative consequences for the individual and their family and contacts. Solvent sniffing, alcohol, cannabis and the whole range of 'designer' drugs affect the lives of millions. Young people, in particular, are at risk from experimentation, escapism from the pressures of life, conforming to social and peer group pressure and seeking the buzz and 'high' experience and confidence which can come from taking drugs. In the highly pressurized world of the 'high flier' there can be a social element to drug taking and the need to escape, let off steam and use the wealth which can come from some jobs.

No-one complains about those of us who go to the doctor to get something to help us sleep. But when this relief turns into a dependency there is concern. Interestingly, no-one disapproves of diabetics, despite the fact that they are not just long-term dependent, but absolutely dependent for life and well-being itself on certain drugs. Obviously there is some distinction between a right and a wrong dependency. A wrong dependency clearly is one that involves physical and psychological risks and can lead to crime, like petty theft, in order to sustain it. While there is debate about the long-term effects of some drugs on bodies as well as minds, it is obvious that drugs do have drastic effects on people. You just have to watch a medical team pumping out someone who has overdosed to realize that.

Drugs have an impact on the health and well-being of individuals and their families and on society. There is a drug culture which can lead into criminal activity and create social problems that threaten the vulnerable, children and young people.

Society's responses

Society is often ambivalent about drugs and sends out contradictory messages. On the one hand, it celebrates the discovery of any new drug which promises relief and cure from disease. It has set up very strict bodies to control the development and use of drugs in medicine, especially after problems caused by drugs like thalidomide and the contraceptive pill. On the other hand, it is deeply and properly concerned about drug abuse in society and the criminal activity which so often accompanies it. Warnings are issued about the dangers of smoking cigarettes, driving under the influence of alcohol and drug abuse. While the media profiles tragic deaths of teenagers from Ecstasy and of popular stars from drug overdoses, it also offers positive pictures of people smoking and drinking and can wink at the use of 'soft' drugs. The police usually ignore small amounts of drugs like cannabis which an individual has for his or her personal consumption, yet they will throw the book at drug peddlers and any hint of drug trafficking. It is this criminal activity, where people are brought into addiction and where money and sex become part of the equation, that concerns society.

Parents are encouraged by television adverts to talk to their children about drugs. Teachers are given information about how to spot both those who are dependent on drugs and those who are likely addicts. Lessons are given in schools to warn young people of the risks involved in taking drugs and the likely effects of drug abuse. There are extensive rehabilitation programmes to try to recover those who have become drug-dependent. The rate of success varies enormously.

Christian perspectives

Medicinal and natural drugs are part of God's good gifts to humanity to alleviate pain, distress and suffering. But like all good things they can be abused and misused. In the Old Testament the laws given to the people of Israel covered every aspect of life and well-being, so it is clear that God is concerned for the health and well-being of individuals and of the community. The descriptions given in the book of Proverbs of the effects of wine might well have been penned to warn of the negative effects of any kind of drug, not just alcohol.

> Who has woe? Who has sorrows?
> Who has strife? Who has complaints?
> Who has needless bruises?
> Who has bloodshot eyes?
> Those who linger over wine,
> who go to sample bowls of mixed wine.
>
> (Proverbs 23:29–30)

> It is not for kings, O Lemuel—
> not for kings to drink wine,
> not for rulers to crave beer,
> lest they drink and forget
> what the law decrees,
> and deprive all the oppressed
> of their rights.
>
> (Proverbs 31:4–5)

The first commandment is to have no other gods (Exodus 20:3), and the danger of drugs is that they can all too easily become a quasi-divine drive to have, to experience and to possess. If our bodies are indeed the temple of the Holy Spirit, we need to be careful what we put in them and how we use them (1 Corinthians 3:16). Paul urges that we do not conform to the pressure of the world around us, whether that is peer group or social pressure. Christians have a responsibility to care properly for themselves and their own bodies and to be aware of the effect of their behaviour and example on others.

Drugs can be used for good or evil, but there are always dangers of physical and psychological abuse and dependency. These can lead to harm to self and others, broken relationships, criminality, poor health and even death itself.

Something to think about

Why am I taking drugs?
Is it under medical supervision?
Am I dependent on drugs for social purposes?
How can I say 'No' to the offer of drugs in social settings?

Is seeking happiness what life is all about?

Background to the problem

Happiness, happiness –
  the greatest gift that I possess.
I thank the Lord that I've been blessed
  with more than my share of happiness.

The lines of this well-known song express our desire for, and pursuit of, happiness. It seems that people not only pursue happiness but are convinced that it is worth pursuing. St Augustine said, 'It is not I alone or even a few others who wish to be happy, but absolutely everybody.' The philosophy of hedonism suggests that we should all seek our own happiness and, in modern terms, do 'whatever turns us on'.

The flip-side of this is the avoidance of pain. Naturally, we withdraw from whatever is painful and seek what is pleasant. Pleasure and pain are the twin gods which guide much of our behaviour. However, there are clear differences over what pleases people in both taste and practice. There are also issues about what limits should be set to the individual and corporate pursuit of pleasure. Are there some pleasurable activities that should be controlled or forbidden by society? At the extreme, we might ask whether sadism and masochism should be left up to the individuals concerned. The problem is that none of us live in a vacuum, and all of us affect other people. One person's happiness may lead to pain for others.

Society's responses

Parents often say that all they want for their children is for them to be happy. Most of us rate happiness at the top of our aims and hopes for life. We also have a very strong sense of 'live and let live' when it comes to different expressions of what makes someone happy. As long as it doesn't hurt someone else, then we are pretty relaxed about what people do in the pursuit of happiness and pleasure.

John Stuart Mill and Jeremy Bentham produced a practical social and legal philosophy, called Utilitarianism, based on the pleasure principle. They argued that in making laws and organizing our life together we should pursue the greatest happiness for the greatest number of people. At its minimum this means avoiding pain and discomfort. At its best it means maximizing happiness for as many people as possible.

There are a number of concerns that arise. Almost everything we do affects other people, and so it is all too easy to harm others by our own pursuit of pleasure. One person's pleasure can easily be another person's pain. Some pleasure seeking can lead to harmful effects like addiction (e.g. to alcohol or sex), self-abuse (as in drug abuse or cigarette smoking), long-term psychological and physical harm as well as short and long-term consequences for other people, like violence and abuse. There is a concern that pleasure seeking is focused only in the short term and really is nothing but selfishness. Even the Utilitarian emphasis is not without its problems, for the pleasure of the majority might mean injustice, pain and discrimination for the minority.

Society does ask whether we should really be trying to avoid all pain, at all costs, both at the individual and communal levels. Should we be encouraging people to be motivated only by pleasure or pain, and, indeed, is this their best motivation?

Christian perspectives

Christians often appear to be killjoys and thoroughly opposed to having a good time. Pleasure is hardly what most people associate with being a Christian. This negativity is sadly a travesty of a proper biblical perspective on the good gifts God has given humanity. God made us so that we have the capacity for pleasure. He has given us a beautiful world, full of good things to enjoy. He has created us so that it is in relationships that we find pleasure at every level – sexual, physical, psychological and spiritual. The Old Testament uses the word *shalom* to cover the sensation, experience, state and aim of our living. It is peaceful pleasure and contentment, where everything and every relationship is in proper balance.

The Bible begins in the book of Genesis with a garden, which is a paradise and a place where there is that perfect balance between human beings, God and the world he has created and given to them to care for and protect. The account of the fall of humanity and the coming of sin into the world pictures the destruction of that paradise, expulsion from the garden and mistrust, hatred and struggle between humanity and God. Inevitably this spills over not just into the breakdown of the relationship with God, but in broken relationships between human beings and with humanity's relationship with the world itself. The story of the Bible – of the salvation promised in the Old Testament and produced by the life and death of Jesus – is a journey from a garden to a city, where there will be no more pain or sorrow, but perfect happiness or *shalom* (Revelation 21:1–4).

It is clear then that happiness is at the very centre of what it means to be a Christian and live a Christian life. The problem is that the meaning and content of pleasure is not the same as secular society understands it. Pleasing God will produce true contentment and ultimate happiness, but it will also involve pain and sacrifice.

Pain is not a good thing, and nowhere does the Bible imply that Christians are to seek pain and suffering. Nevertheless, pain and suffering are real elements in our life and experience. Christianity seeks to give us a means of turning painful experience into something which will produce good. It also provides a means of coping with awful pain and suffering, even when there is no clear good or benefit to be had either for the individual or others. Pain is not to be avoided at all costs or by all means. Indeed, the suffering and pain of Christ on the cross was what brought about salvation and ultimate benefit and happiness for his followers.

The reality of heaven and the eternal pleasure it promises is matched by the awful reality of hell and eternal separation from God. The Bible uses many vivid pictures of fire, punishment and pain to describe what it means to be separated from God and his good care and provision for us. These accounts of heaven and hell should help us focus on what is really important in how we live and the choices we make.

Pleasure, in and of itself, can never be the sole motivation for Christians. God's Word provides a clear picture of our obligations and duties to please God rather than simply to please ourselves. It is in this sense that when we do the will of God, we find true happiness and contentment.

Something to think about

What makes me happy?
Are my pleasures good and wholesome?
What pleases God in what I do?
How do I cope with pain and evil?

2
Social conventions

Everyone does it

Dealing with children can be very instructive. Often when a child is pleading for some new toy, outfit, treat or permission to do something, he or she claims that 'everyone is doing it'. It is interesting that the hassled teacher or parent confronted with a child's plea uses a standard rejection ploy – 'What if everyone did that?' It is clear that what everyone is doing is considered both a justification for doing what we want to do and good grounds for rejecting particular requests to do something.

We are all affected by others, their values, attitudes and behaviour, but should we allow ourselves to be shaped and moulded so much by others? Should we be more independent and accept our individual responsibility? That will mean examining the values and standards around us and asking whether we are willing and able to be different. If we are to avoid being squeezed into the world's mould as Paul suggested (Romans 12:2), we need a more critical appraisal of the impact everyone else has on us and on our behaviour.

Is it all right to be ambitious?

Background to the problem

Typically, ambitious people are those who seek after recognition, promotion, positions of importance and power, and frequently these things involve large amounts of money. They are looking for ways of improving their status in life and, usually, are not terribly concerned with the methods. This self-absorbedness leads to the attitude that others are of secondary importance and that the end justifies the means. If it is necessary to trample on other people in the race to the top, then so be it. For it is far superior to trample than to be trampled on.

Ambition, however, can help people focus on their goals and can be a creative force in helping achieve them. It can enable things to get done, either by personal drive or by enthusing others. The dilemmas arise when aspirations and the desire for recognition outweigh the regard for anyone else. The singular focus and striving to do a job to one's fullest potential are not wrong in and of themselves, but often the means of attaining these goals are dubious. This raises questions about how society copes with conflicting desires and actions, and how it resolves conflicting value systems. It also raises questions about the individual's motivations and treatment of others.

Society's responses

The general response in society to ambition is an affirmative one. Individuals are encouraged to strive and achieve as much as possible because being at the top is what life is all about. Since there is nothing after this world, it is important to extract the most pleasure out of the here and now. Many people seek to make a name for themselves and to obtain power, wealth and fame, for these things enable us to have a high standard of living. Life is seen as a great 'rat race', the survival of the fittest. If some cannot survive, then that is tough luck for them, but they should not expect sympathy from 'the competition'. 'If you can't stand the heat, get out of the kitchen.'

There is no point in looking out for others, as they are all looking out for themselves and it will not do you any good in the end. Of course, you can be over-ambitious, and that turns into greed and carelessness of others. Ambition is good but it has to have some limits.

Christian perspectives

Jesus addressed the issues of ambition, wealth, power, humility and selflessness during his life and ministry. He continually stressed the importance of putting others before self and treating them with care and love, as well as protecting the vulnerable in society. He taught that there was more to life than power, wealth and fame, and that these things are of temporal and not eternal value. What is important is servanthood, which Christ demonstrated time and time again as he served his disciples and others. He gave of himself and did so with a willing heart, setting an example of humility. He was not interested in gaining recognition for himself, and he often instructed people who acknowledged him as the Messiah not to tell others even of the healing he had done for them. Jesus wanted people to recognize him as the Son of God only at the appropriate time, so that they would become part of the kingdom of God and have eternal life. He wanted these things for other people's own good, not to increase his importance or fame in the eyes of the world.

Jesus often came into conflict with the leaders of the Jewish synagogues, people of importance. He did not conform to all of their rules and so was not accepted by them. He often disagreed with their arrogant, ambitious and uncaring attitudes and chose to turn around the rules that made them feel like they were 'above' the rest of Jewish society. He stressed that it was a person's heart and attitude towards God that was the crucial matter, not whether they conformed outwardly to a set of rules. God saw the inside not the outside of a person.

In the Beatitudes (Matthew 5:3–12), Jesus described what a Christian's attitude should be, focusing not on dominating and trampling on other people but on being humble, meek and merciful. He talked about being peacemakers and pure in heart. He also spoke about going the 'extra mile' for others (Matthew 5:41), loving your neighbour as yourself (Luke 10:27) and loving your enemies (Matthew 5:44); ideas which are contrary to the way ambitious human beings treat one another. Jesus stressed that people have a responsibility to take care of the vulnerable in society, not to trample over them.

Jesus did not encourage worldly ambitions because they were motivated by self-interest and material gain. He encouraged people to see the eternal importance of the kingdom of God and be ambitious to further it, not themselves. Jesus also addressed the human desire to store up treasures on earth, both of the tangible kind, like money and property, or the intangible kind, like status and fame. He constantly challenged people to refocus their attentions on the kingdom of God and to store up treasures there where they would be for eternity.

Similarly, Paul suggested that there is a proper ambition for Christians. In Philippians 3, he stressed that we should aim for and have the ambition to fulfil our calling, to be like Christ and to obtain eternal life. We need to challenge ourselves and each other over the nature, content and aim of our ambitions.

Something to think about

What am I ambitious about?
How far am I prepared to go to achieve these ambitions?
Will these ambitions injure others?
Are there Christian ambitions I should have?

What is wrong with white lies?

Background to the problem

President Clinton will probably go down in history for one infamous remark, 'I did not have sex with that woman.' As it turned out, that was a lie, unless you can twist the notion of 'having sex' to exclude what are clearly sexual relations. This is in sharp contrast with another President, George Washington, who, when he was a boy, was asked if he had chopped down a cherry tree and replied, 'Father, I cannot tell a lie.' The problem is whether we can coexist in harmony if we tell the truth, the whole truth and nothing but the truth all the time.

Most people have concealed the truth at some time to ensure that a party or a present was a genuine surprise. Our almost instinctive reaction when we are accused of something is to deny that we did it, even when it is clear that there was no-one else it could have been. When the patient asks the doctor, 'I will get better, won't I?', most of us would expect the doctor to be reassuring. Even if he or she doesn't actually tell a lie, the whole truth is not expressed, and we regard that as justifiable. White lies are justifiable lies for many of us. We want to spare someone's feelings, to avoid embarrassment. We tell 'white lies' when we phone in for a 'sick day' so we can watch the tennis or the football. We think that such lying is part and parcel of being polite and oils the social wheels.

Of course, we can also tell lies to protect other people and ourselves. That might be for good or bad reasons. If you were hiding a Jew from the Nazis in the Second World War, you might lie when the knock on the door led to the question of harbouring 'criminals'.

It looks as if we accept some lies as permissible and others as totally unacceptable.

Society's responses

Society, as so often, wants it all ways. The fact that everyone tells lies at sometime or other seems to justify 'white lies' as long they are genuinely white. If they are to protect others, to avoid unnecessary embarrassment and are purely social conventions, we are tolerant of the 'lies'. If, however, they cause harm or are simply to avoid the consequences of and responsibility for what we have done, they are regarded as wrong. We refine these judgments by looking at the context and who is affected. It may be all right to inflate expense claims if the company is large, has lots of money and does not pay very well. But it is a small step from this to fraud and criminal offences. It looks as if size does matter when it comes to the amount of money or the seriousness of the lie.

Societies do differ. The British were surprised that President Clinton did not resign when he was caught out telling lies about his relationship with Monica Lewinsky. Many Americans seemed more tolerant, accepting that it was proper for him to try to protect his family from the distress of public scandal. In fact, our western world seems to prefer the larger-than-life, risk-taking style of Clinton to what it regards as the priggishness of Washington. The sin is not so much in telling lies as in getting caught. Getting caught undermines the trust that we have in each other. If our politicians, business associates and friends tell us lies, then how can we ever rely on what people say? Our social fabric depends on being able to distinguish truth from falsity and the assumption that most people do not tell lies, most of the time.

Christian perspectives

Satan is described as the 'father of lies' (John 8:44), and so it is no surprise that in the story of the garden of Eden the serpent tells lies that deceive Eve and Adam into disobeying God. Telling lies is catching because Adam then tries to tell God lies and pass the blame on. His son Cain, likewise, tries to deceive God, and so the way that humans tell each other lies is clearly established.

Lying is wrong in itself and brings terrible consequences. Therefore it is inevitable that when God gives rules governing how fallen humanity should try to live in a fallen world, one of the fundamental commandments forbids lying – 'You shall not give false testimony against your neighbour' (Exodus 20:16).

The Psalms and the rest of the Old Testament repeatedly uphold the way of truth and reject lying and deceitful ways. The ungodly are scorned and will reap punishment, while truth-tellers are praised. In the New Testament the example and teaching of Jesus are consistent. Our 'yes' is to be 'yes' and our 'no' clearly a 'no'. There should be no need to take oaths to tell the truth because we are so honest that there should be no doubt about our veracity (Matthew 5:33–37). Jesus was never afraid to tell the truth, especially if it was to confront evil or to force people to face up to reality, as with the Pharisees, the Samaritan woman and the rich young ruler.

In Romans 1, Paul argues that one of the effects of our sin is that we exchange the truth of God for lies. That leads inevitably to destructive ways of living and to social, moral and personal collapse. The clear stress is on truth telling following the example of Jesus, who is the way, the truth and the life. Yet there are some exceptions to the truth-telling rule. Rahab, the prostitute, hid two of the spies sent out by Joshua to Jericho and then lied to the authorities and helped the spies escape. She did this in return for the promise of immunity from destruction when Jericho was taken (Joshua 2:1–6). The writer to the Hebrews commends Rahab's faith in his paean of praise for the heroes and heroines of faith (Hebrews 11:31). It seems that as part of the good purposes of God telling lies from the right motives and within a clear framework of faith may be justified. Such exceptions, however, are not the norm or expected pattern for Christians.

Something to think about

When is it right, if ever, to be 'economical with the truth'?
What are my motives when I tell 'white' lies?
What are the consequences of lying for me and for others?
Are there better ways of expressing difficult things that need to be said?
Do I expect other people always to tell the truth or only sometimes? Why?

Is everyone prejudiced anyway?

Background to the problem

We live in a multi-cultural, multi-ethnic, multi-faith society. It is not just that television has brought the world into our homes, but that increasingly we travel to ever more exotic places. As we walk the streets and eat in the restaurants abroad, we discover other worlds, other races and other cultures. Indeed, we seem quite happy to be surrounded by different races, at least at the level of entertainment and reasonably priced food. As we hear of increasing numbers of asylum seekers, refugees and immigrants, however, we begin to worry about our jobs, our own culture and our traditional ways of life. This is exacerbated when statistics suggest that race is a factor in rising crime. Coping with difference on our doorstep can spill over into riots and violence between racial groups. Our jokes and even the situation comedies on radio and television often reinforce racial prejudices. Once we open Pandora's box of prejudice, we find that homosexuals, Jews, Roman Catholics and anyone different from ourselves become objects of fear, rejection, abuse and prejudice.

Society's responses

Society is quite clear that prejudice is a 'bad thing', but is less clear about what we should do to wipe it out. The law tries to counter prejudice by having racial and sexual discrimination legislation with financial and prison penalties. However, the law sets out only minimum standards. It draws a line below which you may not go in the way you treat, talk about and have dealings with people of different race, faith, sex or sexual orientation. But the law cannot change attitudes and feelings. So society turns to education, with programmes of racial and sexual awareness and cultural studies trying to help us see the world through other people's eyes and to begin to appreciate different customs and behaviours. Such education efforts recognize that human beings are not naturally tolerant and accepting but basically prejudiced. The root of such prejudice is supposed to be ignorance. If we educate and inform people then they will have different attitudes and outlooks. Prejudice can be changed into tolerance.

The primary virtue in western, liberal society is considered to be tolerance, with its live-and-let-live outlook. The ideal is not just to allow difference to exist but to celebrate variety and to insist that everyone learns to accept others.

Christian perspectives

The Bible has two main responses to the reality of prejudice. The first is a diagnosis and the second a prescription. That humanity is by nature prejudiced is part of the truth that all have sinned and fall short of the standards God sets. We always find someone different to blame, fear and mistreat. So the Old Testament offers the beginning of a prescription which commands that the stranger who comes within your home and setting must be respected and protected. If those who were outside the Israelite nation did evil, they were punished. If they lived peaceably, they became trading partners and allies.

The old attitudes of prejudice, however, soon seeped through. The Jews hated the Samaritans and vice versa. Jesus horrified everyone, even his own disciples, by having dealings with Samaritans and Romans. Jesus' encounter with the Samaritan woman at the well (John 4) revealed that he was far more concerned with people than with their race, background, past or behaviour. Jesus responded to people in need.

Paul enshrined this attitude and its underpinning principle when he wrote that in Christ there is neither Jew nor Gentile, male nor female, slave nor freeman, but all are united in Christ (Galatians 3:28). The nail in the coffin of prejudice is for us to look at each other through the eyes of Christ and to realize that there are no fundamental racial, sexual, social or economic distinctions when we stand before God or are part of the kingdom of Christ.

Biblically and theologically speaking, there can be no justification for prejudice when we consider that all human beings are created in the image of God. In that sense, God is the father and creator of all humanity, and this gives equal worth and value to each and every person. Because all are made in the image of God, there is no ground for human distinctions and prejudices against others who share in that image and likeness of God. Equally there is no ground to suppose that any one of us is any better or fundamentally different from others when we accept that we are all sinful people who fail to do what we should and do exactly what we know we ought not to do. If we believe that Christ came and died for all, then we can hardly be prejudiced against people who are different from us. If we believe that one day all will be judged by Christ and that heaven is a setting where people of every tribe, nation and family will be found, then we have no basis for prejudice.

That does not mean, however, that we are to treat any and every behaviour as acceptable. Tolerance does not mean allowing evil to flourish unhindered. Jesus was not prejudiced, but he did respond vigorously to every kind of evil. The nature of his response though is noteworthy for, as with God's punishment in the Old Testament, the point of Jesus' condemnation was always to warn of the eternal consequences of evil doing and thinking and to give an opportunity for change and repentance. Likewise, we must respond forcefully and effectively to evil wherever and in whatever shape it manifests itself, but the aim must always be to restore the person trapped in or expressing evil. Rejecting all prejudice means not prejudging people but giving them the benefit of the doubt. It does not mean tolerance of anything and everything.

Something to think about

Who am I prejudiced against? Why?
What am I trying to do about the roots and expressions of such prejudice?
What would be the attitude of Jesus to such people?
How can I help myself and others to avoid such prejudice?
How may we distinguish between proper responses to people and sheer prejudice?

Are orders to be obeyed without question at all times?

Background to the problem

The Nuremberg trials after the Second World War gave birth to what has become a classic defence excuse: 'I was only obeying orders.' This raises interesting questions about authority and obedience to those who exercise power over us. On the one hand, there is a recognition that if we are part of an official body or organization like the police or the armed forces, or even if we work for an educational or health authority, we are expected to do as we are told and follow the rules and regulations. Otherwise nothing would get done and there would be no consistency or reliability. People would not know what to expect. On the other hand, some orders and regulations are stupid or just plain wrong, and they need to be questioned. Part of helping people develop is encouraging them to reflect seriously on what they are asked to do and to make them part of finding more effective and constructive ways of doing things and achieving aims. Members of organizations are not mere automata, programmed to obey orders without question at all times. The balance between the two attitudes of obedience and critical questioning is the challenge that faces leaders of every kind and in every setting.

Society's responses

Society is, as so often, ambivalent. It despises 'yes' men and women. It often sides with the 'little guy' who takes on the organization over some stupid rule and shows the folly of what was expected. Society also recognizes that organizations can and do get things wrong and so need watchdogs and safeguards. We do not leave business to its own devices. There are legal controls governing business practices to ensure things like price fixing and patterns of discrimination are avoided. We have external checks on professional bodies to ensure that their rules and the application of such rules are fair and just. Openness to public scrutiny is a key concern.

While applauding the individual who takes on an organization with silly or harmful regulations and wins, society is not tolerant of those who break the rules and refuse to follow orders. It accepts that generally people who are in leadership roles are there because they have some expertise and ability. They deserve to lead, and we ought to follow them. Rules and orders are part of the fabric of a society and organization which gets things done. You cannot hope to fight a war or run a school if every command, order and rule is questioned all the time. Behind this realization is the understanding that rules are there for a purpose. They protect people and enable them to function and flourish. The alternative is collapse, where everyone does whatever he or she likes in his or her own way and time.

Authority is a necessary part of society. But that still leaves open the question of who should be given a place of authority. Who should set the rules and who should choose such people? Societies seem to favour the process of electing people because it allows us to get rid of them at the next election time if they fail to deliver, do a good job or keep their promises. Organizations and businesses cannot be run on an elective basis but rely on people with ability and appropriate skills and experience being selected and chosen to occupy leadership roles and high office. Such people are subjected to a very pragmatic test. They either do the job well or badly. If they succeed they tend to be rewarded. If they fail, then they pay the price of failure. We are happy to follow leaders who lead us to success and carry us with them. We are unhappy to obey or follow those we do not respect, or who treat us badly or cannot do the job well.

Christian perspectives

When it comes to obeying those in authority, Peter's appearance before the Sanhedrin sets the standard. When commanded not to speak or teach at all in the name of Jesus, Peter and John replied, 'Judge for yourselves whether it is right in God's sight to obey you rather than God' (Acts 4:19). All authority and power come from God. This means that political and secular authorities have power but it is permitted by God, and they are answerable to him for their exercise of such authority (Romans 13). Those in positions of authority are meant to restrain evil and reinforce what is good. Christians are called to obey, and indeed pray for, those in authority (1 Peter 2:13). It is not, however, a blind obedience. What God wishes and commands must always supersede purely human organizations.

Jesus describes how God has given him all authority in heaven and earth. His exercise of that authority was shown in his life and ministry. Even though he was the King of Glory and could have called down the angelic powers, he refused to force people to obey him, even when it was clearly in their best interests to do so. One of the most remarkable things about Christ was the freedom he gave people to reject him and his will. Such freedom is part of what it means to be a Christian, refusing simply to follow the rules because they are the rules. God gives rules for our good – to avoid harm and to lead to our flourishing. Orders are not to be obeyed without question, but appropriate questioning means testing them in light of God's will for human good and protection from evil. In that way we subject ourselves to the ultimate authority of God and will not only be doing good, but will also avoid any awkward questions on judgment day.

Something to think about

When is it right to disobey orders?
Am I in danger of using my faith simply as an excuse for not doing what I do not want to do?
If those in authority abuse their power, how should we respond?
Should the church be more outspoken in challenging those in positions of power?

3
Sexuality

Sex, love and marriage

A visiting Martian would assume that we are all sex mad in the western world. Society seems to be obsessed with sexuality, and blatant appeals to sex scream from billboards, adverts, magazines and shops. The statistics about sexual behaviour indicate that more people are sexually active, with more partners, at earlier ages than ever before. The wide availability of cheap and relatively safe and reliable contraception has altered our sexual mores. Now it is regarded as the norm to be sexually active, whether or not you are married. It is considered odd to wait for marriage before enjoying sexual relations. Virginity is considered an outmoded idea, and it is thought to be abnormal not to be sexually active. Likewise, chastity seems outdated. Yet being chaste is what is expected for all Christians outside of marriage. Sexual intercourse should happen within the marriage relationship. This reveals something of the 'high' view of the nature of sexual expression.

The consequences in terms of sexually transmitted diseases, HIV and AIDS, unwanted and unplanned pregnancies and the psychological impact of disappointed expectations and ruined hopes are all too real. Young people, in particular, are highly vulnerable to sexual exploitation, and society's revulsion at paedophilia and child abuse shows that we do recognize that sex can be a dangerous activity and drive, which requires control. The problem is how are we to control our sexual urges. As a society, what limits will we allow to an individual's sexual activities? Sexual freedom is not without a price in terms of consequences and requires some accepted limitations.

Why shouldn't I go to bed with someone I love?

Background to the problem

Sex has become a recreational activity. It seems that it has almost replaced shaking hands as a means of getting to know people, except you use different parts of your anatomy and use a little more effort. The expected end of a date is bed. Sex is expected and is just a way of relaxing.

This change in attitude has come about because of the availability of easy-to-use contraception. The contraceptive pill means that a woman can decide to have sexual relations without the likelihood of conception. The widespread availability and use of condoms, initially manufactured for married people, illustrates that sex outside of marriage is now commonplace. Fear of pregnancy is no longer a means of restraint.

While the progression from going out together to ending up in bed seems to have speeded up, that has not been without cost. Sexually transmitted disease is again on the increase. The rate of unwanted pregnancies is also rising, and so too is the toll in disappointment, pain and distress from broken relationships in which both parties expressed a physical commitment that was not supported by a personal commitment to each other.

Society's responses

As long as no-one gets hurt and both parties are willing, society seems to see no problem in casual sex. Of course, suitable pre-cautions must be taken both in terms of the prevention of pregnancy and protection against sexually transmitted diseases. This liberal view stems from a strong sense of individual freedom and the need to banish external restraints. It also rests on the idea that 'everyone does it'. The tradition of waiting for marriage before engaging in sexual intercourse is seen as a guilt trip that needs to be dismissed and replaced by a healthy enjoyment of a relaxing, pleasure-giving activity. Of course, it should be mutually agreed and participated in and enjoyed. There must be no coercion or selfishness in the sexual situation. This seems a little disingenuous given the high rate of sexual abuse of women and rape as well as the tremendous social pressure and social expectation on both women and men to be sexually active. A glance at any young person's magazine, and in particular the problem page, gives the very clear message that sex is normal and a usual part of getting to know someone. Loving someone is about going to bed with him or her.

Society is concerned about promiscuity and the harm done when sexual encounters do not live up to expectations, leaving people frustrated, disappointed and even bitter. On the whole, however, the sexual revolution has been widely and enthusiastically welcomed and endorsed in practice.

Christian perspectives

All too often Christianity has been portrayed, and Christians have behaved, as if sex is evil and dirty. On the contrary, sex is God's gift to humanity. Men and women are sexual creatures, but that does not mean that it is necessary to express that sexuality in a genital way in order to be a man or a woman. Jesus never engaged in sexual intercourse, but he was a real man and fully human. We are far more than our genitals.

God's gift of sex is set in the context of the committed relationship of marriage. First, there is a leaving of the old web of relationships and a cleaving commitment to each other. Only then does the becoming one flesh through sexual union make sense (Genesis 2:24). The validity of this approach is reinforced by the way that most women regard sexual fulfilment as a part of a whole relationship and require a proper sense of safety and security in which love-making can happen. The Song of Solomon is a celebration of human sexuality and the mutual enjoyment which lovers take in each other's bodies when they are already in a committed relationship which alone creates the proper context for love-making.

Traditionally, this high view of the integrity of and respect for the other person was founded not only on love but also on virginity. To be a virgin can be scoffed at and ridiculed, yet our virginity is a gift from God and it is a gift we bestow on the person we marry. That is why we talk of giving oneself in marriage. The integrity of the individual is intact and the specialness of coming to the marriage bed as a virgin makes the beginning of sexual intercourse deeply significant. When a grandmother heard her granddaughter complaining that she was the only virgin in her hall of residence, she kindly and perceptively told her that she could be just like her friends any time she wanted, but her friends could never be like her. She was special.

Christian attitudes to sexual intercourse are based not only on the nature of marriage as outlined in Scripture (Mark 10:6–9; 1 Corinthians 6:12–20; 1 Thessalonians 4:3–7; Hebrews 13:4), but also on the integrity of and respect for the person as a unity of body, mind and spirit. Love is not just about having sex with someone, but caring for the other person and his or her well-being, not just in a few moments of sexual activity but in the context of a life-long commitment. Paul takes the unity that results from sexual intercourse so seriously that he even suggests that having sex with a prostitute makes you one with that person (1 Corinthians 6:16).

It is for good reasons that Christians are called to shun immorality, fornication, evil desires and impurity (1 Corinthians 6:18–19; Colossians 3:5). There is clearly physical and psychological harm which can be done to ourselves and to others by our sexual behaviour. The norm for all Christians is chastity before and outside of marriage. Sexual intercourse should only happen in the context of the relationship of marriage.

Christians are summoned to a quality and expression of love which has captivated the hearts and minds of generations down through the ages. That is partly why the hymn to love in the thirteenth chapter of 1 Corinthians is read at so many weddings. It clearly expresses the true nature of love, which is very different from even the best of one-night stands.

Something to think about

Am I, and is the one I love, more than just a sexual object?
Do I love and respect my partner enough not to have sex?
Is there something special about sexual intercourse and coming to marriage as a virgin?
What is needed in a relationship in order for sex to be meaningful and fulfilling?

How far can a Christian go?

Background to the problem

It is a truism that we live in a society obsessed with sex. Our western culture is one of a high level of sexual activity. If opinion polls are honest and magazines to be believed, then to be sexually active is regarded as the norm and chastity is thought of as abnormal. Traditional values of sex being the prerogative of marriage have been rejected. The specialness of sexual activity is played down, and the Freudian notion that repression of sexual desire is harmful is accepted without demur. It is good to explore one's sexuality. It is also inevitable that two people in a relationship will express that relationship in physical ways. There is an inevitable and totally natural progression from touching and holding hands to full sexual intercourse, with many steps on the way. Indeed, one does not buy a car without giving it a road test first, so it is only sensible to give sex a trial run to make sure that you are really compatible. For Christians, the question remains that if we believe that marriage is the proper context for sexual intercourse, then how far is it appropriate to go physically in a relationship?

Society's responses

We live in a permissive society; so it is no surprise that society thinks that it is entirely natural to progress along a line of increasing sexual intimacy in a relationship. Not only is this natural but it is also considered to be positively harmful to repress those natural physical desires. It is good to express one's sexual, physical nature. It is also inevitable that as people spend a great deal of time together alone, they will find themselves increasingly sexually involved and active. Our natural human desire is to relieve our sexual needs and frustrations and in society's eyes that is a good thing, as long as it is done with consent, is mutually acceptable and does not harm the individuals concerned or anyone else.

Of course, there is pressure from society in advertising, films, magazines and fashion, which all accentuate the sexual elements of dress and behaviour. There is also pressure on each other in a relationship in terms of hopes and expectations. We can also pressure ourselves into going further than we really want and are comfortable with.

In the United States, dating used to be a social activity where a number of couples went out together, thus relieving the pressure on two individuals. This was part of the motive in the practice of chaperoning, where a third party played not just gooseberry but a watching role to reinforce appropriate behaviour. These days are gone, and the back of the car, the bedroom or anywhere else are the settings where people are alone together, vulnerable and responsible. There is all too often the progression from touching to fondling, to stimulation, to undressing, to intercourse and orgasm.

The changes in perception between the generations were demonstrated clearly in the Monica Lewinsky episode. In various interviews she echoed what President Clinton claimed, that they did not have sexual relations. They did engage in oral sex, but they did not regard that as sexual relations. Naturally, there is an obvious difference between sexual intercourse and oral sex, but to suggest that oral sex is not really sex seemed to be stretching the truth beyond what was reasonable. In fact, it indicated very different perceptions about what is or is not permitted and appropriate in terms of sexual expression.

Christian perspectives

Like the rest of society, Christians have become more permissive or understanding about sexual matters. There has been a rejection of the legalism which enforced the 'six inch rule' of no contact or meted out the 'one foot on the floor' advice. Such rules showed very limited imagination and little awareness of the ingenuity of human beings. This kind of legalism did not work and a great deal of cheating took place. The desire for honesty and realism has meant a reconsideration of sexual boundaries and advice.

Christians cannot ignore the special nature of marriage and the role of sexual intimacy and intercourse in the uniting and procreating aspects of the marriage relationship. They should also be aware that sex can be dangerous and addictive, as well as destructive and abusive. We can give in to the pressure from others, to our own sexual drives and to the desire of the other person. Sex is a powerful weapon whereby we can control each other: 'If you loved me then you would . . . '; 'I will let you if . . . '

The question 'How far can a Christian go?' is a bad question. It reveals the mind-set of, 'How much will I be able to get away with before I cross the line?' Rather, a Christian should be asking, 'How can I express my love appropriately and responsibly to my partner before God?' The problem with line-drawing is that it can encourage people to go further than they are comfortable with or to go as near the line as they can manage. Once lines are crossed, it is extremely difficult to go back.

Christians need to recognize the power of sexuality and the significance of each step taken in increasing intimacy from being in a crowd to being alone, from the public to the private, touching to stimulating, clothed to undressed. Because we can all be carried away by our sexual needs and desires, we need to ensure genuine discussion with the other person, to be concerned for their comfort, to be aware of the opportunities and risks of different contexts, and to recognize the force of the heat of the moment. We need also to be aware of the effects of shame and guilt.

There is a fad in the USA which involves badges and bracelets with the slogan WWJD. It asks, 'What would Jesus do?' Beyond the tweeness, there is a serious and important reminder that we are all answerable before God and one good way of considering how far we can go in any area of life is to ask what Jesus would do in that situation. For those of us who do go too far, the good news is that God does forgive us as we genuinely repent and try to live differently.

Christians look to the principles of protecting themselves and other people from every kind of physical and emotional harm. Selfishness and seeking one's own happiness and the fulfilment of desire should be rejected in favour of concern and love for the other person. True love waits. It is concerned to build whole relationships where the physical is in step with emotional, mental, and spiritual development. Sexual intercourse is properly expressed in the context of the life-long commitment of marriage (Genesis 2:24; Matthew 19:3–6).

In his first letter to the Corinthians Paul stresses the importance of self-discipline and self-control (1 Corinthians 6:18–20; 9:27). Perhaps the best advice was given in the paraphrase of Romans 13:14 by J. B. Phillips, 'Don't give the flesh the chance to have its fling.'

Something to think about

Am I concerned for the other person or myself?
What is my/our proper 'comfort zone' for sexual expression?
How can I/we exercise discipline and control?
How would Jesus expect Christians to behave in sexual matters?

Why shouldn't we live together?

Background to the problem

With the evident breakdown of marriages, there has been a move towards living together. Once this was described as 'living in sin', but even the Anglican Church has tempered this language and reflected on how to help people who live together make their relationship work. There are many reasons why people live together rather than marry. One or both partners may already be married and waiting for a divorce to go through. That two can live more cheaply than one is an economic argument for cohabitation. The failure of parents' and friends' marriages has undermined the confidence some young people feel in marriage as an institution. Some reject the institution of marriage in itself and claim that there is more love and commitment when people choose to stay together than when they are forced to do so by an anachronistic practice. For some it offers emotional and sexual intimacy while retaining the independence of being single. For others it offers a 'trial run' and an opportunity to prepare for the real thing of marriage.

Living together is seen as a problem by those who feel that marriage is fundamental to the well-being of a society and that the casual nature of cohabitation arrangements threatens the stability of society and of the relationships themselves.

Society's responses

There is still a little residual embarrassment when being introduced to someone's partner. What's in a name? Generally people are much more frank about their living arrangements than they used to be and regard it as their own private business. As sexual intercourse seems expected much earlier in a relationship, living together seems like the next step down the line in the development of that relationship. As the price of renting and buying property increases, people share to cut cost, and men and women who share a house are not necessarily sexually involved.

At one level, the increase in couples living together is part of a trend which sees that sex is no big deal and just a normal part of getting to know someone and testing out a relationship. If it goes well and people want a greater level of commitment, then cohabitation is an obvious next step. It is better that people try out living together, rather than waiting until they are married to find out that they are incompatible. Parents too have had to become more accepting of their children's various living arrangements. Indeed, society is facing a welter of different living patterns of the same sex and opposite sex partners, divorced and unmarried couples. It is all seen as a natural development in a world where it is hard to sustain traditional ways of relating because of the pressures of modern life. It is also a vote for individual autonomy and freedom. I choose to live with someone or to leave him or her. The choice to stay is made daily rather than simply assumed because we happen to be married. Freedom and true love lie at the heart of cohabitation. While each one can walk out at any point, the fact that they stay is not just a custom or habit, but a genuine choice to be committed to this other person at this particular moment. When children come along then the cohabiting couple usually gets married. They realize that the best context for the having and rearing of children is some kind of marriage relationship.

Christian perspectives

We should always be concerned for the people involved in any situation as well as for the principles and consequences at stake for the rest of us. The sad news is that cohabiting relationships are more likely to fail than marriages. Those who move from living together to marriage are more likely to end up in the divorce courts than those who just marry. These facts conceal the emotional pain and disappointed expectations of thousands. The sheer instability of living together has a serious toll on those who suffer from the broken relationships, all the more devastating because of the intimacy of life together.

Christians believe that God created a marriage pattern, which is not just an individual or social choice and practice, but where God himself and the church play a key role in the preparation for and support of a new marriage. Of course, the church has all too often failed to do a good job, but that is an argument for it to do better rather than one for the rejection of marriage.

It is true that the Bible says very little about marriage ceremonies, but it is clear that marriage was a God-given pattern from the very beginning of humankind and that God is involved in the making and sustaining of the marriage relationship. When the Bible talks of 'what God has joined together' (Matthew 19:6) and compares the married relationship of husband and wife to that of Christ and the church (Ephesians 5:22–23), it is obvious that marriage is more than just something between the couple or within the community.

Christians ought also to be concerned about being free from the very appearance of evil. The challenge for Christians is to live differently and embody the values of Christ. That means resisting the crowd if it advocates something which harms people, goes against God's law and standards or leads people to behaviour which is less than God's ideal.

While the church should be encouraging and enabling those who are living together to be committed and to work at their relationship, there is also the need to teach and show by example that marriage is not just the best place for children, it is also the best place for couples to develop their relationship and have the security and freedom to grow fully.

Something to think about

Why do you think couples live together?
What is wrong with that?
What should the church say and do about cohabitation?
In what ways is marriage better or worse than cohabitation?

How should we respond to the breakdown of a marriage?

Background to the problem

The trend in the West is that more marriages then ever before end in divorce. In 1910 there were 593 divorces in the UK, now there are over 350,000 each year. That fact does not seem to affect the enthusiasm for marriage, for while living together is more common, marriage is as popular as ever. Governments are anxious about the breakdown of marriage, though many feel that they are partly to blame by introducing more permissive legislation allowing 'no fault' divorce and divorce without mutual consent. Marriages break down for a variety of reasons, including the fact that we live longer. We also move job and house more often, leaving the typical and traditional family support settings. Economic pressures and higher expectations of lifestyle often mean that both wife and husband go out to work, a situation which introduces a whole new set of relationships. Affairs usually happen with someone at work. Easier and more available contraception has altered our attitudes to and expression of sexuality, so that sex is more casual and viewed more as a recreational activity. Changing perceptions and expectations of the roles of women and men have affected our patterns of marital relating, so we are often disappointed and bale out of the marriage relationship rather than work at it.

Society's responses

Divorce is a sad fact of life. No-one entering into a marriage thinks that it will fail, in spite of the statistical evidence to the contrary. That very optimism and implicit romanticism may play a role in couples having too high expectations which inevitably will be disappointed. Governments and marriage counselling groups like Relate advise attempts at reconciliation. Relate, in particular, provides support and a framework to work at marriage preservation and, if that fails, amicable separation.

The law has moved in the direction of easier divorce. It has streamlined the process and moved away from the kind of strict blame embodied in the various grounds for divorce towards so-called 'no fault' divorces by mutual consent. The provision has been that there must be a suitable time given to try to make the marriage work and that arbitration help should be sought. We now have the situation where someone can be divorced against their will.

Once society accepts the reality of divorce, the concern is to make it as easy and painless as possible and to safeguard the children and wife. It is usually in that order. One of the effects of feminism has been to stress the equal partnership of marriage, and so if a partner is able to support him or herself then that is encouraged. The assets of the marriage may be divided relatively equally if there are no children. Society holds both parties responsible for the welfare of children. It recognizes that divorce has long-term social and psychological effects on children and that they must be provided for financially at the very least. Often this means going to court for maintenance orders and this adds to the pain and distress of the marriage split.

Once a marriage has ended and divorce happened, society sees nothing wrong with remarriage. It is clear that second marriages are more likely to end in divorce than first ones. Generally, however, there is still strong traditional support for the institution of marriage and an emphasis on preparation for and support of marriage relationships.

Christian perspectives

The Bible teaches that marriage is God's idea. If it were left to humanity we would probably have polygamy or polyandry. Marriage was instituted because man on his own was lonely and incomplete (Genesis 1 – 2). Marriage is meant to be a life-long, faithful, exclusive relationship. The reality is that in a fallen world, sinful men and women fall short of perfect standards. Thus provision was made for divorce in the law of Moses. By the time of Jesus that exception, to cope with the hardness of people's hearts and attitudes, had trivialized divorce until it was permitted on almost any grounds at all. Men could and did divorce their wives on whims. Women were not so free. Jesus was confronted by questions about divorce and remarriage. Different Gospel writers lay different stresses on his teaching. Jesus went back to God's original plan and will, which was that marriage was not just a man and a woman exchanging vows in the presence of an authorized person and witnesses, nor was it just leaving the old set of relationships, 'sticking to' the marriage partner and becoming one flesh for life. God played a role in 'joining' the couple together so that they were no longer two separate individuals but united as one.

In response to the Pharisees' questions about divorce, Jesus indicated that Moses allowed divorce because of the hardness of people's hearts (Deuteronomy 24; Matthew 19). God's intention was for life-long marriage, but humanity is weak and so Moses in the law made provision to help people and society cope when marriages went bad.

The New Testament seems to offer two grounds of divorce. The first is where Jesus talks of divorce on the grounds of *porneia*, a word which refers to some kind of sexual misbehaviour and is the root of our word 'pornography' (Matthew 19:9). Secondly, Paul seems to permit divorce when a non-Christian who is married to a Christian no longer wishes to remain in that relationship (1 Corinthians 7:15). Malachi emphasizes that God hates divorce (Malachi 2:16), and Paul argues in Ephesians that the nature of the relationship between husband and wife parallels the relationship between Christ and the church (Ephesians 5:22–23). Roman Catholics in particular have argued against the possibility of divorce on the grounds of the indissoluble union of husband and wife. Even if the couple separate, they are still one in the eyes of God.

Even the Catholic Church, however, makes a provision for situations when a marriage is not really a marriage and accordingly can be annulled. Such situations include the absence of intention to have children, to be faithful or to regard the marriage as indissoluble. Marriages involving coercion, a lack of discretion, fear, mistaken identity and too close a family relationship are also invalid, as are those not performed by a priest.

For most Protestants, divorce is always less than God's ideal but may be allowed as part and parcel of our fallen nature. The sticking point comes rather with what happens after divorce, and here Christians disagree. Some follow the stress in Mark 10 that to remarry is to commit adultery. Others look carefully at Matthew's exception (Matthew 19:9) and Paul's privilege (1 Corinthians 6:12–16). Both sides in this debate use the New Testament's silence on the matter to argue that remarriage was so obviously practised/forbidden that neither Jesus nor Paul actually state it. Christians will and do disagree about the possibility of divorce and remarriage. The Orthodox Church teaches that after the death of a marriage and a suitable time of separation there may be a new marriage relationship. They would argue that divorce and remarriage are not unforgivable sins.

What all accept is that the church must offer good quality marriage preparation and support, adequate help and care for those whose marriages are breaking down and are suffering in those situations, along with positive assistance in making relationships work, whether these are old or newly established ones. Divorce and remarriage are not unforgivable sins in spite of the message sometimes expressed. The challenge for Christians is to live and proclaim God's ideal pattern of marriage, but also to be prepared to offer loving support when things go wrong.

Something to think about

Why do marriages break down?
How can I help myself and others avoid such breakdowns?
How can I protect all those affected when a marriage ends?
Should the church remarry divorced people?
If not, how should we respond to people who are divorced and remarried?
If so, how can we help marriages, especially second ones, flourish?

How should Christians regard contraception?

Background to the problem

There are too many people in the world. If we look at population growth in the developing world, it is clear that we are rapidly running out of space. Governments and international agencies are engaged in a massive drive to limit the size of families. Where there is no provision of social services or old age pensions, then a large family is one way of providing for parental needs into old age. The idea of contraception is culturally suspect in some settings, and many people have religious and aesthetic reasons to reject contraception. At the same time, population levels in the West have, until very recently, been falling. More couples are delaying childbirth or rejecting it all together. They are spacing their family in order to maintain a high standard of living for themselves and for any children they have. Having children is a costly business.

At the same time, patterns of and attitudes towards sexual behaviour have changed dramatically with the arrival of safer, relatively reliable contraceptive measures. The link between sexual intercourse and procreation has been broken; sex is more of a recreational activity and pregnancy is to be avoided at all costs and by any means.

Society's responses

Society has welcomed the arrival of safer, more successful contraception. The changing role of women and feminism have moved the world of contraception from risky, doubtful potions to a more scientific world of condoms, caps, pills, coils, injections and temperature charts. What was originally designed to help married couples space their families is now available for all, single or married. The sexual revolution means that we can all engage in sexual activity without fear of the consequences of an unwanted pregnancy. Contraception, however, does not guard against sexually transmitted diseases like syphilis, gonorrhoea, HIV and AIDS.

The main concern about contraception in the West is safety and availability. There is debate about the provision of contraceptive advice and accessories in schools and colleges, but generally unwanted pregnancies and possible abortion are regarded as much more evil than sexual activity. There is also concern about the safety of certain oral contraceptives in relation to women's health. While there may be a slight benefit in relation to cervical cancer, there is greater risk of heart problems.

In the wider context, society is concerned about over-population and supports moves to make contraception widely available in countries where there is no tradition of small families. There is, however, horror at moves to use abortion as a late contraceptive or, in settings like India and China where the preference is for boys, at the practice of aborting female foetuses very late in the pregnancy. In contrast, the morning-after pill has been hailed as a means of providing emergency contraception when none was used or there was a contraceptive failure. The French health authorities provided high school girls with morning-after pills over the Christmas holidays because the clinics would be closed.

There is little awareness, far less concern, about the way that contraceptives work. That some act as an abortifacient, expelling fertilized eggs, seems of little importance to those seeking reliable contraception. As long as the one using the contraceptive is safe, anything seems permitted.

The current advances are looking at providing male contraception by injection to avoid any unpleasant aesthetic interruption in sexual matters. At the extreme, male or female sterilization is a means of contraception, but this depends on a clear decision that childbearing is over. However, no contraceptive, not even sterilization, is 100% effective. On the other hand, there have also been cases where frantic attempts have been made to reverse sterilization after the death of a child or when a new relationship has begun.

Christian perspectives

Children are regarded as a blessing from God in the Old Testament. God is seen as the one who opens or closes the womb, and fertility and its control lie in his hands (e.g. Sarah, Rachel, Hannah). In Genesis God commands humanity to be fruitful, multiply and fill the earth (Genesis 1:28). This command was repeated after the flood (Genesis 9:1). Some regard this as a mandate arguing against contraception. On that basis, however, Jesus was guilty of breaking the commandment because he neither married nor fathered children.

Obviously, modern means of contraception are not mentioned in the Bible. There is a reference to the so-called 'withdrawal method' in the story of Onan, where the act is described as 'wicked' (Genesis 38:9–10). The sin of Onan, however, was not *coitus interruptus*, but his moral and social failure to fulfil his obligations to his dead brother's name and inheritance by providing him with an heir (Deuteronomy 25:5–10).

Christians ought to be concerned about the motives and nature of contraception. A concern to protect the wife from the rigours of pregnancy and childbirth, to provide properly for any children one has or to limit the population in the world are very different motives from refusing to have a child so that one can enjoy a particular lifestyle. Likewise, using post-intercourse methods or abortions looks like a desire to escape the consequences of engaging in life-creating activities. Christians are not only concerned about the impact of contraception on the woman but on the fertilized eggs. Some techniques like the coil, high oestrogen drugs and the so-called morning-after pills act as abortifacients expelling fertilized eggs. If we regard human life as beginning at the moment of fertilization, when the whole of the genetic code is in place and, other things being equal, that child will develop into a person as we are, then this is taking innocent human life. This is explicitly forbidden in Scripture (Genesis 9:1–6; Exodus 20:13; Deuteronomy 21:1–9). Christians need to know exactly how each contraceptive works so that they can then draw a distinction between preventing fertilization and ejecting an already fertilized egg.

Roman Catholics have argued against all forms of artificial contraception on the grounds that it goes against God's natural law. While it is hard to define what is now 'natural' in light of medicines and our fallen world, Catholics are deeply concerned to protect women and children. They support natural family spacing, using self-control and the so-called safe period when women are not fertile. The latter is not always easy to determine and the unkind refer to it as 'Vatican roulette'.

Christians recognize that the proper context for sexual expression and so contraception is marriage. The Bible teaches that 'leaving and cleaving' are to come before becoming one flesh (Genesis 2:24; Matthew 19:4–7). Our sex-obsessed society reverses the order. Children, young people and society need to be protected and to realize that early sexual experience has serious consequences. It is no small matter to give contraceptives to people without explaining their function and risks as well as trying to help people understand that sexual expression needs a context of the loving committed relationship of marriage.

There is also a need to consider the consequences of using various forms of contraceptives both for the woman and for the embryo. The taking of innocent life is undoubtedly an evil. While it is clear that there are moral consequences of using contraception, it is important to recognize that there are also consequences of not using contraception. The balancing of motives, consequences and the nature and function of each kind of contraception requires Christians to reflect thoughtfully and biblically on what is right.

Something to think about

Are there legitimate forms of contraception?
Are there illegitimate forms of contraception?
Why do we want to use contraception?
How are we to regulate, if at all, the giving of contraceptives to young people? Why?

What is wrong with being gay?

Background to the problem

Homosexuality has a long tradition going back to Plato and beyond. It is the physical, sexual attraction to the same sex and occurs in both the male and female. The incidence of homosexual practice is a matter of debate. Many, following Freud and Kinsey, argue that everyone passes through a stage of homosexual attraction as a part of growing and developing. It is simply a stage, but some get 'stuck' there. Others regard it, not so much as a 'natural' stage or activity, but a choice of lifestyle and behaviour. The number of people who are exclusively homosexual in their orientation and practice varies from estimates of 10% to 2%.

It is clear that many in single-sex situations do engage in homosexual activity and that many heterosexual people perform the same sex acts as homosexuals. Thus our modern world faces a problem at two levels. Individuals are not always happy if they think that they are homosexual and often look for help in overcoming their desires. How are we to respond to those who are struggling with their sexual identity? Concern for young people as they develop their own sense of sexual identity and may suffer from confusion and be vulnerable to influence has led to a difference in the age of consent between women and men which is still debated. This seems to indicate a view that women mature earlier than men and are more quickly settled in their sexual identity. The fact that the law interferes at all shows that society does regard homosexuality as an issue, not least in the prejudice and discrimination against homosexual people. This can be expressed at the level of the words and humour we use or the stereotyping of homosexual people.

There is a growing distinction within the 'gay' community about whether it is best to adopt a low profile, simply getting on with relationships, or else to be provocative and challenge society's attitudes and norms. Such demands for equal 'gay' rights include an end to discrimination in employment and an equal portrayal of homosexual and heterosexual relationships in school literature to encourage and enable young people to choose their own sexual identities. There are even moves to legitimate marriage between homosexuals. Certainly the law, insurance and employment practice has moved in the direction of recognizing the stability of homosexual relationships and the entitlements that follow from that.

Society's responses

As so often, society is ambivalent. In theory, freedom of expression and tolerance of difference is the ideal. As long as no-one is forced or hurt then homosexual activity is accepted. Indeed, some argue that the quality of some homosexual relationships and the benefits for those involved is high. Love is the necessary and sufficient condition for practice. The opposite view is that there is some kind of perversion at work here and homosexual behaviour is abnormal. Prejudice and discrimination against 'gay' people is rife and takes many forms ranging from the snide comment to the violence of 'queer bashing'. The threat of HIV and AIDS has reinforced negative attitudes towards homosexual people, even though this is usually based on a misunderstanding of the causes and transmission of those diseases.

At root there is a good deal of homophobia (literally, 'fear of the same') and anxiety that somehow homosexual people are more likely to seduce young people and to threaten 'normal' heterosexual people. In reality, some heterosexual people engage in oral and anal sex, so the activities of homosexual people themselves cannot be so easily dismissed as abnormal.

There is considerable debate about the definition and causes of homosexuality. Often there is confusion between the activity and nature, desire and action. Claims that there is a genetic base for homosexual behaviour seem unsubstantiated. Family background, early sexual experience, choice and physical characteristics may all play a role in the development of homosexuality.

Christian perspectives

Christians need to repent of homophobia, prejudice and a lack of loving concern for homosexual people. There has been a great deal of confusion between rejection of certain practices and rejecting the people who engage in them. That is the point in suggesting that we are to love the person while hating the sin. The church has been increasingly divided about the propriety and significance of homosexual behaviour. Nowhere is this more evident than in the Anglican setting, where it has been argued that homosexual behaviour can be condoned among the laity but not the clergy and that practising homosexuals ought not to be ordained. At the same time the Anglican Communion world-wide has condemned homosexual practice as plainly against the will of God. The reality is that there are many homosexual people at all levels in all denominations.

While the church has shown the same kind of fear of homosexuality as society, it has also tended to make sexual sin seem more serious than other kinds of sin and homosexual practice the worst sin of all. There is no biblical or theological ground for such a view.

While Christians are called to love others, this is not the same as condoning or accepting everything that anyone does. The Bible has clear teaching about homosexual practice, but there is a debate about the contextual nature and authority of this teaching. Some try to argue that it was only written for those particular situations and times and is not relevant today. Others claim that it is possible to interpret each passage as condemning only promiscuous homosexual activity. This is stretching the plain sense that the majority of serious commentators accept. The Bible condemns homosexual practice.

The foundation of the Bible's stance stems from the teaching in Genesis that marriage is the proper context for sexual activity. Marriage is between male and female. The stories of Sodom and Gomorrah (Genesis 19:1–29) and the men of Gibeah (Judges 19) and the levitical laws (Leviticus 18:22; 20:13) indicate God's denunciation of homosexual activity. This is picked up by Paul in Romans and 1 Corinthians, where sexual sins are included in the condemnation of sin in general (Romans 1:24–32; 1 Corinthians 6:9–11). Paul is equally clear that some of the Corinthians had been homosexually active in the past but had now changed and were living very different lives.

Christians can only point to God's standards and seek to help all of us live by those standards. For many Christians who think and feel that they are homosexual by inclination and orientation, the only option is to be non-practising. We do not need to be sexually active to be fully human.

Something to think about

Am I concerned about my sexual orientation?
Am I prejudiced towards homosexual people?
Do I believe there is a difference between orientation/attitude/desire, and engaging in an activity?
How can I help all of us who struggle with sexual temptation?

Is AIDS the punishment of God?

Background to the problem

The frightening discovery of AIDS (Acquired Immune Deficiency Syndrome) in the early 1980s caused both panic and prejudice. The early cases seemed to indicate that AIDS was a 'gay plague' and this caused concentration on exploring the possible causes and cures and steps towards prevention especially in relation to the homosexual community. There was a tremendous change in the behaviour and practices of that group as the life-threatening nature of AIDS and the link between the disease and sexual activity became clear. The general public, which had become much more tolerant of homosexuality and its public expression, reacted with fear and prejudice. Some religious leaders argued that AIDS was, in fact, a punishment from God for homosexual behaviour. This caused outrage in both the 'gay' community and the rest of society. What kind of God punished people in this sort of way? How did he act in the world to bring this punishment about?

It is estimated that there will be 40 million sufferers from HIV and AIDS in the world by 2020, including both heterosexuals and homosexuals. The enormous health, financial and social implications for those who will have to live with the disease and for their families and communities means that we will have to rethink our attitudes and strategies in relation to prevention, care and cure.

Society's responses

We have been increasingly distanced from death in the modern world and so the reality of the unexpected physical decline and death of a largely young population was all the more shocking. Soon it seemed that all of us knew someone who had died from AIDS. Sadly, this initially included people who had received infected blood transfusions or blood products. These people were regarded as 'innocent' victims, in contrast to those who 'deserved' what they got because of their behaviour and sexual activities. As it became clear scientifically that HIV and AIDS were passed on by intimate contact of body fluids and that it was a sexual disease rather than an exclusively homosexual disease, society's attitudes modified and changed. The gap between the infection and the development of full-blown AIDS meant that society had to provide care for those suffering. The shift from seeing the disease as a western problem to the realization that vast numbers of people were at risk in Africa and Asia, in particular, raised all kinds of moral questions about health-care resources, prevention, sexually explicit advertising, and our responsibility for humanity. Resources have been poured into AIDS research, but there is little prospect of a cure.

The fear of HIV and AIDS was all the greater because they seemed to threaten us at our most vulnerable as human beings in the context of sexual intimacy. This fear often expressed itself in a return to prejudice, particularly against 'gay' people. This was not helped by the reversion on the part of some homosexuals to practices which had been abandoned as a result of so-called 'safe sex' campaigns. It was as if homosexuals after being tested and found negative for HIV thought that they could safely return to high-risk sexual practices. Scare stories in the press reinforced prejudice and fear.

On the other hand, the 'gay' community organized a level of care and self-help for AIDS sufferers which put to shame the inadequate medical and personal provision by society and the churches. Christianity was dismissed as unloving, judgmental and destructive. The notion of God interfering was laughed at and lampooned. Christian love seemed strangely absent.

Christian perspectives

Christians must confess that some of the initial reactions were indeed lacking in love and understanding. In considering how to reflect on AIDS we need to focus on how we understand the nature of God. Pictures of a divine being sitting in heaven making AIDS thunderbolts and throwing them down to earth with such poor aim that the 'guilty' are often missed and the 'innocent' made to suffer are a travesty of God and his relation to the world.

God is a God of love who created the world we inhabit and made humanity in his image. God is also a moral God who sets standards for human behaviour that are not whimsical but are designed for the good and flourishing of human beings and life. God has designed the world and human beings so that certain ways of living are good in themselves as well as good for people, and other ways are harmful. In the same way, if we go against the revealed will of God then there is an inevitable price to be paid (Leviticus 26:3–17). What we sow we reap (Galatians 6:8), and there are inevitable consequences if we misuse or abuse our bodies. It is, therefore, no wonder that the Old and New Testaments warn against sexual immorality, knowing the terrible effects that can result. AIDS is a disease largely transmitted by sexual means. Sexual intimacy with one faithful partner is the only guaranteed way to be safe.

Christians must reflect, however, whether they are guilty of homophobia in their initial reaction to AIDS. Homosexual practice is clearly condemned in Scripture (see 'What is wrong with being gay?'), but there is no condemnation of homosexual people. Sexual sin of any kind is not worse or better than any other sin. All sin is sin and serious in the sight of God. All sin carries consequences in both the here and now and the there and then.

We are all sinners, but we do have a Christian responsibility to warn those who are at risk and to care for those who are affected by their sin. The creation of Christian hospices to care for those with HIV and AIDS is a proper, if belated, response to human tragedy.

In making a careful case that all our behaviour has consequences and results, Christians need to beware of the wrong kind of judgment which is really prejudice (Matthew 5:22; Romans 14:10). In John 8:11, when Jesus was confronted by the woman caught in adultery, he neither condoned nor condemned her, but he did warn her to leave her life of sin. Perhaps Christians also need to look again at their attitude to and beliefs about death and to use appropriately the certainty of life after death as a way of bringing hope to those facing the reality of death and dying.

Something to think about

Do I believe that what we sow, we reap?
Do I believe that AIDS is a direct punishment from God?
How can I help people with AIDS?
How can I avoid prejudice and judgmentalism when it comes to those with AIDS?
How can I protect against AIDS?

4
Women and men

Men are from Mars, women are from Venus

The battle of the sexes takes many forms, and our modern culture has seen the rise, and perhaps the fall, of feminism. The impact of two world wars, changing economic and social patterns and the development of relatively safe and reliable female contraception have helped create and foster a philosophical and moral shift in women's attitudes to themselves and in male–female interactions and perceptions. Women have increasingly taken control of their own lives. Patriarchal rule has been slowly but surely eroded. In the workplace, women have taken top jobs and, in most cases, have gained equal pay for equal work. There has also been a reaction against some of the extremes of feminism, and in areas like medicine and business there are still all too few women in the very senior roles.

All of this has created pressure on both women and men. Women are expected to be successful in the boardroom, miraculous in the kitchen and fantastic in bed, as well as keeping the home immaculate and the children well-adjusted. Their relationship with men is less clear than the traditional, hierarchical pattern demanded. Part of the problem is that men are not sure what it means to be a modern man. They are now not just allowed to cry in public but are expected to do so and to be deeply responsive to the needs of a woman without needing to ask what is the matter. They are also expected to be the strong, protective, macho man much beloved of the action moviegoer. Rambo is alive and well and at times still very attractive to women. What then does it mean to be a woman and a man in our world and how should we relate to one another?

A woman needs a man like a fish needs a bicycle?

Background to the problem

Throughout history, male-dominated society has viewed women as the 'weaker' sex and assumed that women need sheltering and protecting from the outside world. Within and outside the home, men were ultimately in charge, though women had an important role in home-making and having and caring for children. From the Victorian era to the 1950s and beyond, society has thought of women as less capable and more susceptible to harm than men. Women were seen as ruled by emotion and feelings, while men were ruled by rationality. While women cared for home and hearth, men were hunter-gatherers out in the world, earning a living.

Since the 1970s the feminist movement has developed, stressing that women have a worth and status at least the same as that of men. This movement has tried to expand the choices and opportunities that women have in life, from careers to relationships. At the same time it has challenged societal views and the treatment of women. To facilitate these aims, feminists have advocated the use of non-sexist language and created an atmosphere of 'political correctness'. While there is a wide range and variety of outlooks and attitudes within feminism, at its extreme some radical feminists have embraced not only lesbianism, but a rejection of men from every activity, including sex and procreation.

This has inevitably led to a reaction to feminism by both women and men. It has been dismissed by some as a misdirected ideology and they have tried to keep traditional gender roles in place. Others have tried to distil the key emphasis of putting right the 'abuse' of power and women by men to create a more equal society. It must be wondered how far feminism has been genuinely successful in changing the attitudes, behaviour and perspectives of women and of men. While political and employment patterns are more sensitive to women, their rightful place and opportunities, there seems to be a reversion to type in terms of relationships and marriage and family expectations and roles.

Society's responses

What is the proper relationship to be between women and men? Where people begin is crucial. There has always been definite and continued discrimination against women in every sphere of life, even if there has been improvement in the last few years. Women now have more and better career opportunities but still hit the glass ceiling of middle management, with limited salary and promotion prospects. Remarkably few women hold senior roles in medicine, politics and on corporation boards. Many women are expected to continue their work at home as well as their external job, without any significant shift towards genuinely shared responsibilities with their partners.

On the other hand, there have always been those who place a proper emphasis on women's rights, demanding that women be viewed as full and equal members of society, with the same freedoms, privileges and opportunities that men enjoy. Feminists, both male and female, claim that women have been discriminated against and now is the time to rectify these wrongs.

Christian perspectives

The creation pattern of the relationship between men and women is one of complementing each other and being companions. Man on his own was incomplete, and women and men are able to support and fulfil each other. The picture is one of mutuality and reciprocity, with women and men as equal partners who were equally created in the image of God and have the same worth and value. The fall changed all that. Relationships were broken. Because of disobeying God's command, humankind began to blame each other, refused to accept responsibilities and had to face the awful consequences of sin and brokenness. Eve would experience pain in childbearing and her desire would be for her husband and he would rule over her (Genesis 3:16). Life changed for Adam, too, and became one of toil and a struggle to survive (Genesis 3:17). Both were banished from the garden paradise and no longer had direct communion and contact with God. The pattern of man's dominion over woman was not God's original desire or intent. It was only after the fall that human beings distorted the roles of women and men into being hierarchical and imbalanced.

Jesus' ministry is a clear example of non-hierarchical relationships between women and men. He overrode many cultural and traditional norms to relate to women directly, even those of so-called 'ill repute'. John 4 recounts Jesus' meeting with the Samaritan woman. This story reveals the crucial way Jesus challenged the norms, expectations and discriminations of the day. He spoke to the woman without any hint of superiority and clearly related to her as an equal. The records of the New Testament reveal that women were the key witnesses to the events of the cross and the resurrection, at a time when in legal contexts women's evidence was discounted. The emphasis in the New Testament is revolutionary in the treatment and inclusion of women both in ministry and in the meeting of individual needs. Jesus restored a proper relationship between the sexes.

Of course, there are heated discussions over the meaning and application of difficult passages, including 1 Corinthians 11 – 14 and 1 Timothy 2, where notions of submission and hierarchy are the nubs of the debate. Whatever these passages mean and how they are to be applied, there can be no doubt that women and men are not only equally created, but also equally redeemed and destined for glory. Salvation and wholeness for the human community must mean a wholeness and restoration of proper relationships between women and men. The church is the context where we must learn how to relate in ways that complement both sexes and enable everyone to be fully the man and woman God created and destined them to be. While there are crucial differences between women and men, in Christ there is no distinction, or room for discrimination, between men and women (Galatians 3:28).

Society needs both sexes to fulfil their varied gifts, callings and natures. We, as Christians, need to do this together under the lordship of Christ who calls husbands and wives to mutual submission to him (Ephesians 5:21). Proper relationships must involve mutual respect, care, love and the constant aim of helping everyone grow into the full humanity God intends for all human beings.

Something to think about

What does it mean to be male and female today?
Are the differences between the sexes important for the roles and ways of relating people have?
Are we guilty of sex discrimination?
How are we to interpret and apply the 'difficult' passages about male and female relationships?
What do mutuality and reciprocity mean in practice for relationships between women and men?

What does it mean to be a man today?

Background to the problem

The rise of feminism has created tension for many men over their role and identity. Are they to continue to be macho men full of testosterone and aggression or should they manifest their feminine side and be gentle, caring, sharing companions? The problem is that society and women seem to be demanding both. It is all too easy to get it wrong and to fail to be the kind of man a woman wants when she wants it. Traditionally men have been stereotyped as aggressive, driving, ambitious, hunter-gatherers, who are sex mad and only interested in themselves and male-bonding drinking sessions watching sports. Now there is a new man, who is in touch with his feminine characteristics, gentle, communicating, concerned not just about the environment and world issues, but deeply committed to allowing and enabling women to be themselves. He not only eats quiche, but makes it, shares in all the household chores and is willing to be a 'house husband' if the woman wants to develop her career and the children need to be looked after in the home.

Society's responses

An end to men's aggression in war and in sexual violence against women in rape and abuse is welcomed by all. Patriarchy is at an end, and the power of men over women has to be destroyed. The problem is what exactly to put in its place. This is harder when the behaviour of some women is just like that of men at their worst. The 'ladette' culture seems to glorify women getting drunk, lusting after male bodies and generally behaving in uninhibited, outrageous ways. The world of films and television still often portray desirable men as tough, self-contained, sexually predatory, forceful and action based. At the same time, women are increasingly expecting men to be freer in expressing their feelings and sensitive to women and their particular needs and desires. Men, however, are not very good at intimacy and have a fear of commitment and an inability to communicate what they are feeling and to be sensitive to women. It is no wonder that many think that men are from Mars and women from Venus.

Many men fear feminization. They are afraid that they will be labelled 'homosexual' if they show the softer more sensitive side of their nature. Such fear can manifest itself in anti-gay jokes and even extreme behaviour like 'gay bashing'. Where men are insecure about their own sexual identity they often behave in ways designed to 'prove' their masculinity. At the same time, gay men are increasingly accepted as having an alternative lifestyle in society. Men can choose and express their own sexual preferences. There is also a growing 'pink market' where the homosexual community is targeted in advertising. This spills over into general male concern about appearance. Increasing numbers of men spend more and more time and money on exercise, hair products and even make-up. The 'body beautiful' applies equally to men and women as an aim to be pursued.

The traditional settings for masculinity in war and playing aggressive sports have been largely replaced by watching sport in front of the television or from the stands. Sadly, most violent crime is still committed by young men. When poor education and unemployment are added to an identity crisis for young men, violent behaviour is often the result.

There are, however, moves in a different direction. Men may be taught how to cook, but the reality is that when it comes to sharing a home together men refuse to do more than token housework and expect the women not just to have a successful job but to cook, clean, look after the children and be a whiz in bed. Failing in relationships manifests itself in more men staying single and living with their parents until their late twenties.

Christian perspectives

Men can be defined as what women are not. The model for manhood, and indeed personhood, is Jesus Christ. He was the perfect man, who lived a life for others in obedience to God. It is no surprise then that when Paul is trying to stress how men should behave, especially in relation to their wives, he looks to the example of Christ. Not only are men, like women, to be imitators of God (Ephesians 5:1), they are also to give them the same sort of love that Christ gave to the church when he sacrificed himself for her (Ephesians 5:25–26). This is no easy option but a pattern of self-sacrifice and service of others as witnessed in Jesus washing the disciples' feet (John 13).

The problem for Christians is centuries of failing to take the example of Christ seriously and of particular interpretations and applications of key biblical passages. There is wide debate about the meaning of 'headship' and 'submission' in passages like 1 Corinthians 11:3–16 and Ephesians 5:22–23. Many men have regarded this as an excuse for domination, but this is to misunderstand God's pattern of male relationships with women. Not only are men and women created equal and made in God's image, but the breakdown in their relationship was a result of the fall. It was only after the fall that the equality, mutuality and reciprocity of the garden were twisted into patterns of domination. Paul is clear that men and women are to submit to one another out of reverence for Christ (Ephesians 5:21). This is no charter for the exploitation of women. Men are to regard women in light of their own submission to Christ. 'How would Jesus act towards others?' is a key guiding theme. The Gospel records show how Jesus never threatened women but elevated them and treated them with love and respect. He was the man for others, and that pattern of service and self-sacrifice is the essence of true humanity and thus of masculinity. It is not tied to sexual behaviour, for there is no record that Jesus ever engaged in any sexual relationship. Yet he was fully man and fully human.

The way for men to discover who they are in the twenty-first century is not in isolation from other men or from women. All of us need to explore what it means to be human, male and female with each other. We can then develop and encourage patterns of behaviour and personal traits which allow us to be fully ourselves in constructive and good relationships with each other, all in light of our relationship with God.

Something to think about

What do you think are the characteristics of being male?
Why are some men so anxious about their identity?
How has feminism helped and hindered men's sense of who they are?
How can we develop a positive view of what it means to be a man in Christ?

What is wrong with being a feminist?

Background to the problem

The very expression of the question indicates that feminism has not been universally welcomed. It rose to prominence in the 1970s partly as a reaction against a long history of oppression and discrimination against women by men. Feminists believed that men had occupied positions of power and control and had used that power to control women, denying them opportunities and equality, and making them serve the ends of men. Women were meant to be 'pregnant, barefoot and in the kitchen'. So women were denied access to higher education, jobs, promotion and public involvement in decision-making. Feminism challenged this kind of discrimination and argued for an end to such stereotyping and positive discrimination to allow women to make their own unique contribution on their terms.

As well as fighting patriarchy, feminism fought for women's rights. In the USA the focus was on the Equal Rights Amendment, trying to ensure equal rights and opportunities for women. This was accompanied by a stress on the sexual freedom of women. Men had long been able to enjoy wider sexual freedom and relationships than women, but with the advent of female forms of contraception women gained greater control over their own bodies. That led to the idea that a woman has a right to do whatever she wants with her own body, and the right to choose an abortion without having to explain or defend that decision became the touchstone of the feminist movement.

Some feminists almost rejected men completely and engaged in lesbianism. For them ideas of marriage, traditional patterns of childbearing and rearing needed to be replaced. Far more women emphasized the feminine sense of community, the importance of women-to-women dialogue and support and the distinctive female approach to thinking, relating and acting that would enhance public decision-making. By being 'connected', women would be able to resist oppression and to find alternative strategies to enable them to choose what they wanted in life and what forms their relationships with women should take rather than simply being at the mercy of male oppression.

Society's responses

In the mixture of society's responses, the proper stress on women's rights and the need to redress the balance in the male–female relationships was largely welcomed. The benefit for many women has been new opportunities in education and access to the higher paid, more responsible jobs. Perceptions of womanhood have been challenged and to some degree changed, so younger women in particular have broader expectations about what they can achieve. However, while there may have been some progress, there are doubts about the real depth of success in achieving full equality and overcoming all forms of discrimination. Whether men's, and even women's, fundamental attitudes have been altered is much debated. Many women regard getting married and having children as their key role; the goal to be pursued regardless of all the worthy talk of female equality.

Inevitably, there was a rejection of feminist views, not only by men but also by some women. They believed that society was fine when men went out to work and women stayed at home. They argued that the status of women is in fact undermined by feminism and the result is a brutalization of society. Traditional male and female roles have served humanity well and do not require fundamental change. Even some who initially supported feminism have either been distressed by the 'extreme' views of some feminists, or have felt that feminism has achieved its aims and now the problems have been solved and there is no need for further struggle.

Christian perspectives

My feminist friends tell me that God made Adam first and then thought he could do better so he created Eve. In fact, you do not need to twist the first few chapters of Genesis to realize that woman was created because man on his own was incomplete – 'It is not good for the man to be alone' (Genesis 2:18). Woman was created to be a helper and partner for man. They were equally created in the image of God and intended to complement one another. Two sad consequences of the fall were that women tended to be blamed for it and the open relationship of equality became a battle between the sexes.

It is clear from the Old and New Testaments that Adam was fully responsible for sin and its long-term effects, and that blaming Eve was no excuse. The reality now is that women and men have to struggle for a proper way to relate.

Women in the Old Testament were often in positions of importance and authority. Miriam was clearly a leader in the Exodus story (Exodus 15:20–21), and Deborah was a judge over Israel (Judges 4:4). The contrast with other cultures and the role and contribution of women are celebrated in books like Ruth. God used women and men to accomplish his purposes. In the giving of the law, women were to be protected and cared for, especially the widow. The community had to provide for those who were vulnerable.

Unfortunately, some of the application of the law had undermined the worth and status of women. Easy divorce is a key example, where men mistreated and abused women, divorcing them on no real ground at all. Jesus reversed that, not only in the respect and care he personally showed to women, but in the close friendships he made with women, like Mary and Martha, and his public dealing with women which many found offensive. Women were the key witnesses at both the cross and at the empty tomb. It is no surprise then that Paul argued that in Christ there is no male or female (Galatians 3:28).

Feminism properly rejects domination and oppression. Christians must oppose all such behaviour and institutional forms of prejudice. The claims and proposals of feminism need to be taken seriously, but there are some moral concerns to be expressed. No-one has total freedom over his or her own body. We must not replace one kind of domination with another form. Rather, we need to explore what it means to be female and male in the context of the church and in the context of God's plan for complementarity.

Something to think about

What is right with feminism?
What is wrong with feminism?
Which of feminism's claims and proposals should be accepted and which rejected?
In what ways would Jesus be considered a feminist today?

5

The wider world

The whole world in our hands

Christianity has had an ambiguous, changing relationship to and with the wider world. Initially the world seemed a hostile place liable to contaminate Christians, yet needing salvation and a saviour. It was a world to be won and converted. With the conversion of Constantine and the creation of the Holy Roman Empire, Christendom was set up, where Christianity was more integral to every aspect of life and rested at the very heart of government and power. In the Reformation the possibility arose of the separation of church and state into two kingdoms where different rules and strategies were appropriate. We now live in a setting where there is a close church–state relationship, which is constantly being debated from inside and outside the church.

Christians are partly of the world and need to ask what their role is in that wider world. Is it simply a setting for evangelization and missionary activity? Is it part of God's good creation and final consummation of history and therefore to be cherished? How is it possible to behave as salt and light in a world which does not share a belief in God, an experience of Christ and an openness to the Holy Spirit? What does it mean to live as women and men in our world today?

Is God on the side of the poor?

Background to the problem

What it means to be poor used to be seen simply as lacking in the basic necessities of life. If you are poor then you can barely survive, far less flourish. Poverty in this sense is the lack of food, water, shelter and the means to survive. The meaning of poverty has been extended to include not just this sense of absolute poverty and hardship but a sense of relative poverty. Compared with those others who have a good standard of living there are people who are deprived of what is regarded as basic to live at all reasonably in a society. This is not a matter of life and death but of comparative poverty and deprivation. There may be such a poor quality of education, housing, employment (if any at all) and access to the whole gamut of services which are part and parcel of modern life that people so affected are genuinely poor, disadvantaged and deprived.

As members of one world we have some kind of responsibility for the poor in both senses. Often we are responsible for some poverty, at least indirectly, by the policies and practices of governments and businesses we support. We also allow things to happen and do little or nothing to prevent injustice and the creation of poverty. This is clearly a waste of human potential. There is always the possibility of a threat from those at the bottom of the pile in a society and thus self-interest alone would seem to support the need for action to limit or eliminate poverty.

Media pictures and well-organized campaigns like Drop the Debt and Jubilee 2000 have drawn attention to the awfulness of poverty and its devastating effects on the lives of individuals, families and nations. The success of these campaigns is that people have been moved to give and to work to eradicate poverty.

Society's responses

The awareness of the dangers to the stability of a nation, or even world trade, by the presence of large numbers of poor people who may be driven to extreme action by their condition terrifies some people into action. The idea that the poor can pull themselves up by their own bootstraps is not as unreservedly believed as it once was. The sheer scale of the problem and the very helplessness of people trapped in a cycle of poverty drive us to the conclusion that individual or even corporate charity is not enough to make a difference. Traditionally, charitable giving was the cure for poverty based on the belief that if you give people a helping hand, they will be able to make it in society and get out of poverty. This is clearly not the case. It is not just that poverty demotivates and destroys people, but that it is institutionalized and drags down those who are in settings where all the hard work and willingness in the world will not make a difference.

Governments and business have been driven to the recognition that the practices of world trade and development aid need serious overhaul. Too often aid was given in return for a requirement of trade, often at extremely unfavourable terms for the recipient of the aid. International business has moved manufacturing from relatively expensive western settings to places where labour is cheap and even child labour is used to keep down the costs. Exposure and public awareness has driven business and governments to look again at trading and aid conditions and to seek to be more sympathetic and constructive in dealing with the causes of poverty.

Similarly, nations, agencies and governments have tried different strategies to alleviate poverty. There has been a shift from simply giving help to creating opportunities for education, training and employment to enable people to escape from the poverty trap.

In all honesty, there are still people who think that poverty is the fault of the poor and that poor people are just feckless and lazy. While there are lazy and feckless people in every setting in society, that is no reason to refuse to create the conditions where people are able to make a difference in their own and their family's lives.

Christian perspectives

Jesus foretold that there would always be poverty (Mark 14:7; John 12:8). This is no excuse to accept poverty. God is clearly concerned about the poor. Poverty is harmful in that it isolates people (Proverbs 14:20; 19:4, 7), it leaves them at the mercy of the rich and powerful (Proverbs 18:23) and it dishonours the God who made us (Proverbs 14:31; 17:5). The Bible is shot through with commands to give generously to the poor (e.g. Proverbs 31:20; Isaiah 58:7; Matthew 5:42). The Mosaic law provided for the release from servitude of those whose poverty had driven them into slavery (Deuteronomy 15:12), and land was to be returned to its original owner in the Jubilee Year (Leviticus 25:28). Those who do give to the poor will be rewarded (Psalm 41:1–3; Isaiah 58:10; Jeremiah 22:16; Luke 14:12–14). The old, the sick, the widowed and the fatherless were special objects of God's concern and were to be for all the people of Israel.

In the coming of Jesus these same commands were not just reinforced but exemplified in his life, teaching and ministry. He came to the poor and lived as a poor person (Matthew 8:20–22). He sent the disciples out in poverty and humility (Luke 10:3–4). The most scathing attack on the failure to meet the needs of the poor is contained in the parable of the sheep and the goats (Matthew 25:31–46). The way we treat the poor and needy reveals our spiritual state in this life and the next. Jesus, however, identified poverty not just in material terms. He stressed that there is a poverty of spirit and came to meet the needs of both kinds of poverty (Luke 18:23–25; 19:1–10).

The gospel from the start was 'good news to the poor' (Luke 4:18) and the church is called to meet the needs of the poor, not just by charitable giving, but by serious engagement with the causes of poverty. Inevitably, that means talking to businesses and government about policies and practices which harm people and keep them trapped in poverty. Sharing the good news of the gospel must go hand in hand with meeting the material needs of those who suffer.

Something to think about

What are the causes of poverty in our world?
To what extent are we to blame by what we do and fail to do?

Is relative poverty as serious as absolute poverty?
What should be done about both?
What characteristics of the poor does the Bible commend?

What can we do about hunger in the world?

Background to the problem

In developing countries one child in every ten dies before the age of five and one sixth of the population – almost 800 million people, one quarter of them children – are malnourished. It is not only hunger that kills. Each day over 30,000 children die from preventable diseases like diarrhoea, malaria or respiratory problems. In the last fifty years almost 400 million people have died from hunger. That is three times the total number killed in all the wars in the twentieth century.

Life expectancy, quality of life and even survival itself are affected by hunger. We live in a world where all too many have too little food. That is aggravated by famine, which strikes nations like Somalia and causes widespread human death and destruction. It also stands in sharp contrast with western affluence and over-consumption. A visit to any restaurant in the USA will show an individual's plate piled high with enough food to feed one family. People feel that they have been short-changed unless they are able to ask for a 'doggy bag' to take away the food that they have not been able to eat.

Governments continue to spend massive amounts on weapons instead of on health, education and maintaining a decent standard of living for all the citizens of the world.

Society's responses

When a crisis happens, as with famine in Africa, society is generous in its response. 'Feed the World' was not just a song designed to raise money for hunger relief but the catalyst for a series of attempts, like Comic Relief, to inform the public and encourage them to give to help overcome starvation. Oxfam and many other secular and religious groups have long been active in helping sway public opinion and government policies to help the problem of hunger in the world. The aim is not so much to give aid, though that is part of the agenda, it is more to change the trade and economic policies of the affluent nations. The aim is also to encourage individuals in their own lifestyles and shopping habits to be concerned about the producers of food and other goods and their poverty.

Hunger is clearly related to poverty. Poor education and desperation exacerbate this. Hungry people cut down trees and bushes as fuel. This causes deforestation and loss of fodder for animals, which leads to a spiral of famine and environmental destruction which makes farming impossible.

Western societies will give aid, but it is often tied to economic opportunities for the donor country. Countries with large international debts may grow crops like coffee for western markets where payment in hard currency will mean possible repayment of debts. Such crops may be of no help to the hungry nationals who are producing the coffee rather than growing their own food.

Aid agencies have shifted attention away from simply alleviating hunger itself to dealing with the causes of hunger and poverty. Giving someone a fish may feed them for a day, while teaching them to fish will feed them for a lifetime. Self-help patterns of good agriculture and environmental practices are increasingly encouraged. Population growth is also being addressed. Limiting family size, and therefore need and demand, is a key factor in overcoming lack of food.

There are, however, those who blame countries for their own predicament. They point to the outrageous greed and behaviour of dictators and those in power, who line their own pockets rather than meeting the needs of those they serve and represent. There is still a 'pull yourself up by your own bootstraps' mentality. The problem is that western patterns of democracy and of response to disaster are not the norm. When people are at the mercy of natural disasters and unjust rulers, it is up to the rest of the world to respond compassionately based on our common humanity.

Christian perspectives

Christian Aid, Tear Fund and Cafod have been key Christian leaders in responding to the hunger needs of the world. They have shown Christian love in action not simply by giving emergency aid but in building long-term programmes of survival, good farming and environmental practice, health education and skills training. They have also been active in lobbying governments and trade organizations to be more generous and to change their economic and trade policies. Jubilee 2000 is a classic example of a partially successful campaign to drop the debt requirements on poorer nations to allow them to redirect their finances and trade to help their own people.

Such practical policies rest on the fact that men and women are all made in the image of God. Their worth and value demand that we respond to human need. The story of God's dealings with Joseph in Genesis 41 illustrates God's providential concern in a famine situation. Joseph was raised to high office not only to help the Egyptians but also to save and preserve the children of Israel.

Jesus came not only with the good news in word but also in deed. He fed the hungry, having compassion on their physical need (Mark 6:32–44; John 6:1–13). He rejected the disciples' suggestion that it was the responsibility of the hungry to feed themselves, but rather he took what was available and used it miraculously to feed everyone and still have food left over. The feeding of the hungry takes on eternal significance in the parable of the sheep and the goats. It describes how reward and punishment are awarded not on the basis of whether or not a person claims to follow Christ, but on the basis of whether or not that person has put Christ's compassion into action.

The early church provided food for those who were unable to provide for themselves (Acts 4:34–35; 6:1–4). This was carefully planned and organized so that not only were needs met but justice was done. Paul recounts the excellent example of the Macedonian churches responding to the needs of the famine-stricken church in Jerusalem. They gave in such a self-sacrificial and generous way that others should follow their pattern (2 Corinthians 8:1–15). His principle seems to be that those who have much should meet the needs of those who have little, and when the situation is reversed the pattern of care and giving will too, so that there will be equality. Paul's appeal is both to the generosity inspired by the example of Christ and an awareness of self-interest.

The challenge for Christians is to support agencies with special expertise in helping meet the hunger needs of the world. We need to encourage governments to give appropriate aid and embark on just economic and trade policies. At the same time we should adopt a lifestyle and pattern of consumption which shows regard for the needs of others. We ought to live simply so that others may simply live.

Something to think about

Why is there a problem of hunger in the world?
What is our responsibility as human beings for others?
What is our responsibility as Christians for others?
How may we live more simply so that others may simply live?

Why should I be concerned about the environment?

Background to the problem

The environmental problem can be summed up as too many people consuming too much of the world's resources. The ozone layer is being destroyed, and global warming means a serious change in weather patterns, soil erosion and water levels. Land is being degraded so less is available for crops and creatures. Erosion, salinization and desertification are the results. Industrial and chemical waste are polluting the water we drink and the air we breathe. Rain forests are being destroyed to create cash crops for financially needy nations trying to satisfy the consumer desires of richer, western nations. Plant and animal species and raw materials are fast disappearing. Biodiversity is at risk. We are literally poisoning our world with too much rubbish and the indiscriminate use of pesticides, fertilizers and insecticides.

There are too many people in the world, especially in the developing nations. The First World – you and I – are consuming too many of the world's resources and wasting what there is. Technology is out of control. BSE and foot-and-mouth disease are prime examples of the price we pay for putting profit and production first. Genetically modified foods and intensive farming practices have caused a backlash against new technologies.

At the same time, we are running out of wilderness, and our national parks and green spaces are over used and abused. There is clearly an environmental crisis of massive proportions.

Society's responses

Society is increasingly concerned about the environment. Nations are making treaties like the Kyoto Protocol to try to restrain chemical emissions and protect against global warming. The moral basis for concern is threefold. Many environmentalists appeal to selfishness, claiming that we are running out of world and our standard of living is beginning to suffer. The air we breathe, the water we drink and the land we use are all affecting our health and living in negative ways. Animals and plants are disappearing and may never be recovered. We are running out of natural resources and so prices of energy and food costs will rise and we will no longer be able to afford to live as we do today. We need to cut our consumption now.

There is also an appeal to our responsibility for future generations. We were given a well-stocked world and it is our task to safeguard and protect that for our children's children. We should pass on to future generations a world in which they will be able to live well and flourish.

Some have argued, based on what is called the Gaia hypothesis, that the world is a biological unity and everything we do affects every other part of reality. As thinking guardians of nature, we have a responsibility to ensure that there is proper respect for the world and its natural patterns. We should be working with nature to protect our environment. That means a change in personal, social and international attitudes to life, farming, animals and nature itself. Radical adaptations in demand, consumption and lifestyle are required if we are all to survive. Otherwise we and the world will die together.

Environmentalists recognize that there are economic forces at work in national and international settings and that these need to be controlled. This requires reliable scientific information about the causes and cures for our environmental woes. Currently not everyone is convinced that the problem is so serious and that such drastic measures are required.

Christian perspectives

Some argue that Christianity is to blame for the ecological crisis. The commands to be fruitful and multiply and to subdue the earth and have dominion over it are seen as charters for abuse and exploitation (Genesis 1:28). The population crisis and rejection of contraception have meant that we have too many people. Technology in the hands of those who followed a Protestant work ethic and believed that prosperity was a sign of God's blessing, encouraged people to abuse the world for selfish ends. Terrible farming and chemical testing methods simply to serve human needs have abused animals.

These are serious charges, but they fail to look sufficiently carefully at what the Bible teaches. Humanity was indeed given dominion, but that in no way implies domination. Rather in the Old and the New Testaments such dominion is always under the lordship of God. Human beings are responsible and answerable to God for their use of the world and its resources. The world and all that is in it belongs to God. We are simply stewards of God's good gifts. As stewards we are entitled and invited to enjoy the world and live off what has been given. We are not entitled to abuse the world or animals simply for our own ends.

After the flood, human beings were allowed to eat animal flesh (Genesis 9:3) and, as happened in the fall, our relationships with nature were fundamentally altered. Instead of a garden paradise where there was plenty, humanity would have to struggle against nature to overcome it and to eke out a living (Genesis 3:17–19).

None of this denies that we have been guilty of environmental abuse, but Christianity is not to blame, rather human greed and selfishness. Old Testament laws dealt sympathetically with the land and animals. Human beings were meant to have care for what God had given. That same note of stewardship is evident in Jesus' teaching, especially in many of his parables. We are answerable to God for what we do and what we fail to do. Talents are given to be used appropriately and God is our judge (Matthew 25:14–30).

Practically speaking, Christians need to be informed about the dangers of the ecological crisis. We need to examine our lifestyle and our patterns of consumption so that we can guard against greed and selfishness. Increasingly, recycling has become part of proper stewardship. A concern for animals means treating them appropriately and protecting them from abuse. The Genesis account clearly shows that human beings are more important than animals, and it is proper to use animals for food, clothing and to prevent harm to humans in medical research. That is no charter for cruelty and carelessness about the conditions in which animals are bred, kept and killed.

Christians should join with those who are concerned about the environment without becoming worshippers of nature and having a false sentimentality about the animal kingdom. The earth is the Lord's, and in the beginning there was a close relationship between humanity and the heavens and the earth. This will be restored at the end of time and if we believe in a renewed creation as pictured in Isaiah 35 and Revelation 21 – 22, then we should continue to be good stewards and care for a world which is yet to be fully redeemed.

Something to think about

Why is there an environmental crisis?

Is Christianity really to blame?

How do you evaluate the three main secular arguments in favour of environmental concern?

How are we to live as Christians who are concerned about our world and all that is in it?

Why should I love my black, Jewish, crippled, gay, elderly, and mentally handicapped neighbour?

Background to the problem

Racism, sexism, ageism are all forms of discrimination. We live in a world where there has always been discrimination against those who are or seem different. People of a different nationality or race, colour, sex or sexual orientation or with different physical or mental abilities threaten us by their very difference and by the need to respond to them. The obvious differences of race, sex, sexual orientation, colour, age and physical ability cause us not just to stare but to treat others as inferior. This negative discrimination means that such people may be denied full and free equal access to many basic necessities of life such as education, employment, housing and health care. Both personally and institutionally, society discriminates against groups and individuals. This both bolsters the status and preferential standing of those who are 'acceptable' and consequently have power and refuses access to the basic necessities safeguarded by 'civil rights' to those on the outside. We feel revulsion against such racism, sexism and ageism until a black, Jewish, gay, elderly, mentally handicapped person moves in next door and threatens to take the jobs of people like us.

Society's responses

Modern societies are convinced that discrimination on the grounds of race or sex is wrong and needs to be corrected. The effects of discrimination mean that women earn less than men do and that coloured people have less access to health, employment and educational opportunities. Racial violence is on the increase in major cities, and religious and national stereotyping reinforces patterns of fear, hatred and discrimination.

Society's cure is at two levels. Legislation against discrimination has grown in the last fifty years. Racial and sexual equality and the rights of disabled people have all formed part of anti-discrimination laws. Employers and statutory authorities are forbidden to discriminate against anyone on grounds of race, colour, ethnic origin, nationality or gender. Such laws have been extended to include the creation of opportunities for recruitment, promotion, employment and access to services and benefits. People with disabilities are likewise not to be discriminated against in terms of employment, pay and opportunity. The United States has gone a step further in not just forbidding discrimination but creating affirmative action programmes and opportunities through positive discrimination. This means that in work or education settings there will be a bias in favour of the placement of women or members of particular racial groups. The law or constitution is meant to be colour and sex blind. Thus new laws seek to ensure that employment and access to housing, health care and other social services are in no way denied to minority groups and individuals.

While the law may change discriminatory practices, there is still a problem over the attitudes of people. In an attempt to change such attitudes governments have embarked on extensive education initiatives designed to foster understanding of minority groups and encourage people to regard others as equal and entitled to the same rights and privileges as all other members of a society. At the heart of both prongs in the attack against discrimination lies a belief in human equality and the need for fair and equal treatment for all.

Christian perspectives

God created all women and men equal. From the beginning, there was equality in terms of creation and by being made in the image of God. While man was created first, it is clear from Genesis that man on his own was incomplete, and that there was no distinction between men and women in that it was God who created them both. Different races and sexes share a common heritage and heavenly father.

Likewise, all human beings suffer from the effects of sin. Genesis 3 outlines the fallenness of human relations in terms of male dominance and female subservience. The sinfulness of human relationships is shown throughout the Old Testament, where relationships between people threaten the very existence of Israel and there is the need to preserve the nation from outside influences. God commanded his people to exterminate his enemies. Yet even in the midst of such awful judgments on other nations, God commanded the people of Israel to care for the stranger and the foreigner. In Deuteronomy 26:11 God commands that the alien and the stranger should benefit from his goodness to his people. All oppression and affliction are to be resisted and the needy cared for regardless of who they are (Psalm 72:4).

Christ revealed God's love for all humanity. 'For God so loved the world that he gave his one and only Son, that whoever believes in him shall not perish but have eternal life' (John 3:16), shows the universal nature and significance of God's love and Christ's death and sacrifice.

Jesus condemned discrimination. His command was not to pass judgment on others (Matthew 7:1–6). He rebuked the Pharisees and even his own disciples for their attitude towards Samaritans and people of other races. The parable of the good Samaritan (Luke 10:25–37), Jesus' encounter with the Syro-Phoenician woman (Mark 7:24–30) and the healing of the centurion's servant (Matthew 8:5–13) challenged racial prejudice.

Paul sums up the significance of this in Galatians 3:28. When we realize what Christ has done for humanity, this removes any basis for sexual or racial discrimination. In Athens Paul proclaimed the common humanity we all share (Acts 17:26). This was not easy for the early church to accept, but in the Council of Jerusalem (Acts 15) we see the recognition and practice that the gospel is for all and no human distinctions should hinder that.

Unfortunately, the church has not always been opposed to prejudice and discrimination. However, the example of leaders like the Earl of Shaftesbury and Martin Luther King shows Christianity should oppose discrimination. Christians are called not simply to help remove discrimination from the practices of a society but to change the hearts, minds and attitudes of people. This is the way to ensure that we really do love our black, Jewish, crippled, gay, elderly and mentally handicapped neighbour.

Something to think about

Why do we discriminate against others?
What can be done about that in society?
How can we begin to change our own attitudes?
Is the church guilty of institutional discrimination against women and people of other races?

6
Life

Making babies and manipulating people

Many modern medical discoveries centre on the beginnings of life. Fertility and genetic research has produced key breakthroughs in understanding infertility, helping infertile couples have children and clarifying the link between genetic make up and certain diseases. Such research has also created some brand new moral problems as well as refocusing attention on long established ones. Philosophers and theologians have always struggled with the question of when life begins, and now biologists are offering a very different perspective. New moral problems arise when we separate procreation from sexual behaviour in marriage. How are we to define what is a parent? What rights and responsibilities do donors of eggs, sperm and wombs, and the children born from such artificial means, have? What limits, if any, should be set on who may have fertility treatment or receive contraceptive advice and devices? The more we study the beginnings of life the more we are confronted with fundamental questions of what it means to be human and what we mean when we talk of persons.

When does life begin?

Background to the problem

Fertility treatment and improved contraception has led to greater understanding of the beginnings of life, but not to agreement about when life actually begins. Fertilization, when the egg and the sperm unite, is the likely first point. Because there is up to 40% loss of such early embryonic life, the moment of implantation, when the fertilized egg fastens to the womb, is often preferred. This option allows the use of the Intra-Uterine Device, the morning-after pill and certain forms of the contraceptive pill which expel fertilized eggs and prevent them implanting on the side of the womb. The Warnock Committee opted for fourteen days as the beginning of life, after which it should be protected. That is when the primitive streak develops. It becomes the central cortex and controls the body–brain interaction. It is also the point when each embryo is now an individual and can no longer divide into twins. For the woman, the moment of quickening may be the choice, because then independent life and movement is directly felt.

The medical profession prefers viability as the defining factor in deciding when life begins. This is currently about twenty weeks, as high technology medicine is able to preserve a child's life outside the womb at this point in a special care baby unit. However, this is a sliding scale and indicates more about our capacity to sustain life than life itself. It is also under pressure because of the increased performing of *in utero* surgery, where the clear benefit is for the child, even if the operation takes place 'through' the mother. The moment of birth, when the child takes his or her first breath is for many the time when an individual's life can be said to begin. Joseph Fletcher of 'Situation Ethics' fame argues that life begins when you are independent of your parents, which speaks volumes about the status of students! Jokingly, for many life really begins when the children leave home and the dog dies. The reality is that there is no agreement about when life begins.

Society's responses

It seems that the nearer to the moment of birth and viability, the more society recognizes and treats the child as a person requiring the protection of the law and appropriate responses from us all. In the past, when a child was stillborn its body was disposed of in the incinerator. Now the child is clothed, pictures are taken of the parents holding the dead child and there is a naming ceremony and a funeral. This shows a better understanding of parental grief and the attitude towards human life as it becomes more like us. The law likewise seems to recognize that life within the womb deserves some rights and protection. In cases of injury to the new life in the womb, parents can sue for damage and loss. If the child is born handicapped because of an accident when in the womb, then the child is able to sue on his or her own behalf. Obviously, the abortion law fully protects human life only after twenty-four weeks, but the requirement that abortion be limited to situations where it is justified on health grounds indicates that human life is in some sense being protected.

In contrast, society seems little interested in embryonic life, unless there is some direct involvement. A couple losing embryos designed for fertility treatment or having a miscarriage feel the pain of personal loss. It is their child, or their best chance of having a child, that has been lost. There is little concern and often little understanding about the use of IUDs, the morning-after pill and other forms of abortifacient contraceptives. There is usually delight when a pregnancy is confirmed but no consistent attitude towards human life from the earliest stages.

Christian perspectives

For Christians, the psalmist sums up the wonder and significance of human life within the womb.

> For you created my inmost being;
>   you knit me together in my mother's womb . . .

My frame was not hidden from you
when I was made in the secret place.
When I was woven together in
the depths of the earth,
your eyes saw my unformed body.
All the days ordained for me
were written in your book
before one of them came to be.
(Psalm 139:13–16)

Human life is special and sacred because we are made in the image of God. God creates humanity, and we are privileged to act as co-creators in the conceiving and birth of children. The prophets Isaiah and Jeremiah point to God's call of them even before they were conceived in the womb (Isaiah 44:2–5; Jeremiah 1:5). Luke, the physician, recounts the reactions of Elizabeth and her child in the womb, John the Baptist, to the coming of Mary, newly pregnant with Christ (Luke 1:41).

It is clear that human life is special from its earliest stages. Any view which takes 'earliest stages' to mean 'from conception' will rule out certain abortifacient kinds of contraception, drawing a distinction between methods that prevent fertilization and others which expel fertilized eggs. It will mean that choices in fertility treatment will exclude the creation and disposal of 'spare' embryos with no regard for their status and significance. And it will mean that thoughtful and appropriate care will be given to those who have had miscarriages or stillbirths, especially in the disposal of the remains.

Modernity rejects any discussion of when the soul enters the body, and Christians do well to avoid the split between the physical and the spiritual. The New Testament is concerned for the whole person. The problem is that modern understandings of personhood and personality do not easily fit with the biblical record. Christians need to remind society of the special nature of human life and the need to protect the vulnerable and to match that concern with a Christian witness and lifestyle which shows in practice how we treat human life. We need to be consistent about contraceptive, fertility and obstetrics choices and how we react when foetal life is lost.

Something to think about

When do you think human life begins?
What significance does that have?
How can the church be more consistent in the way it deals with early foetal loss?
What implications does your view of the beginning of life have with regard to methods of contraception?
What kinds of fertility treatments should Christians be concerned about?

Should we use embryos for medical research?

Background to the problem

One result of fertility treatment has been the creation of 'spare' embryos. Most drugs given to help women conceive cause super-ovulation, the creation of many eggs, which can be frozen or fertilized. This allows embryologists to select the 'best' embryos for implantation. As a result there are spare embryos and these can be used for experimental work. Initially, such research was restricted to fertility and infertility. This has been extended as the science of genetics has taken off and the link between disease and genetics has become clearer. Recent developments with stem cells taken from embryos offer scientists the hope of new treatments, particularly in the area of Parkinson's disease, organ transplantation and diabetes. This controversial technique removes cells from an embryo, thus ending the embryo's life. These stem cells can be recreated to make stem cell lines and thus there is a body of material for experimentation. Adult stem cells can be removed easily, but it is feared that such stem cells are not as effective, malleable and as likely to be successful in creating new organs, tissue and cells as those from embryos.

Society's responses

Faced with new biotechnological advances, the British government formed the Warnock Committee to draw up guidelines. This has blossomed into the Human Fertilization and Embryology Authority. It oversees and regulates what is permitted not only in fertility work but also in embryological research.

Experimentation is permitted on embryos up to fourteen days old. That is when the primitive streak develops, which becomes the central cortex, and you thus have one individual. Experimental work needs permission and is subject to regulation.

Society welcomes fertility work which helps couples who are desperate to have children, but are unable to do so. There are, however, a host of moral problems created about single, lesbian and older women having access to such treatment. Many complicated issues result concerning what is a parent, donor rights and responsibilities and a child's right to know his or her genetic parents.

The discovery of stem cell research and the possibilities it offers excites the public. Tragic high-profile cases of Parkinson's disease like Michael J. Fox create an enthusiasm to proceed with research into a cure at all costs. However, stem cell research does involve the ending of human life and thus the status of the embryo lies at the centre of the debate. Society does not value the embryo as highly as sick adults and children. It argues that abortion is already widely accepted and that here is a way of using material from the aborted baby to bring relief to suffering people. The end justifies the means, especially when the end is so worthwhile and the means has happened for another good reason.

Christian perspectives

Christians have a responsibility for the vulnerable and those who are unable to speak for themselves. Christians also have to recognize that secular society does not share their values. Our task, therefore, is both to proclaim God's moral standards and to find winsome ways of persuading society to act and regulate medical research appropriately.

Christians are uneasy about the techniques of super-ovulation, the consent for and use of material from aborted babies and the disposal of embryos. If life begins at fertilization, then we are dealing with human beings. Of course, such a human being is not yet the same as an adult, but it is clearly human and will become exactly like us, other things being equal. We recognize that other things like miscarriage may intervene. From the psalmist's words in Psalm 139 to the accounts of the calling of Isaiah and Jeremiah (Isaiah 44:24; Jeremiah 1:5) and Luke's accounts of John the Baptist and Jesus in the womb (Luke 1) we can see God's involvement and concern for foetal life. The commandments against the taking of innocent human life (Genesis 9:5–6; Exodus 20:13; Deuteronomy 21:1–9) should make us hesitate to kill embryos. Some Christians argue that if death has already happened, as in an abortion, then we should make good come out of evil and use the aborted baby to help others. This can appear to justify the act of abortion and seems like an argument where the end justifies the means. It does not seem to offer respect to the dead and would justify using the bodies of executed criminals for medical purposes.

More cogently, some regard the development of a person from embryo to child as increasingly and gradually requiring more protection and involvement. They point to the pastoral practice where the baby from an early miscarriage has traditionally not been named, buried or christened. This practice is changing in hospitals as the loss and grief of parents is recognized and consistency with the status of early human life is required.

In the United States, President George W. Bush has agreed to fund stem cell research only in cases where there is an existing stem cell line (i.e. when an abortion has already happened) and so there will be no justification for taking further human life. This is a compromise which upholds the sanctity of human life by refusing to fund research where human beings will be created only to be destroyed in the pursuit of science. It does, however, allow scientists access to the sixty existing stem cell lines which can replicate indefinitely. Scientists complain that this will limit research. Christians have responded that there are alternative approaches in the use of adult stem cells which are likely to be successful. They are fearful that scientists in their zeal for discovery, success and finance may have exaggerated the likely benefits and the time-scale involved. Concern exists also about the role of pharmaceutical companies and their pursuit of profit and the lack of adequate regulation of the research that does happen, particularly in private clinical settings where no rules seem to apply.

Good quality, enforced regulation is vital to restrain evil. In weighing the benefits and the costs, many Christians will be concerned about the devaluation of human life and the easy use of others without their consent in medical research. Trying to persuade society of the value of embryonic life is not easy, but it requires consistent living, ministry and engagement.

Something to think about

What is your view of the status of the embryo?

Do you think that aborted babies should be used for research purposes?

What limits should be placed on the funding and regulation of medical embryological research?

How can Christians show consistency in their attitudes towards early human life?

How can Christians persuade a secular society to value humanity at its early stages of development?

Can abortion ever be justified?

Background to the problem

There have always been abortions, but modern medicine has refined and hospitalized the process, and the law regulates the circumstances. Before 1968 over 600 women a year were dying from botched back-street abortions. The 1968 Abortion Act allowed abortion under certain circumstances: two doctors had to agree; there had to be a risk to the life of the mother, or to the social, economical or psychological well-being of the mother or other members of the family; or else the predicted quality of life of the baby was so poor that abortion was justified in law. All this was supposed to happen before the twenty-eighth week of development. Now there are over 300,000 abortions carried out each year, and what was initially permission has become an expectation. We have in the UK and in most of the USA what amounts to abortion on demand.

Medical and contraceptive developments have led to new dilemmas with the so-called morning-after pill, which acts as an abortifacient by causing the expulsion of the embryo. Fertility techniques of implanting multiple embryos lead to 'selective reduction' involving killing the 'spare embryos'.

Abortion arouses great emotion on both sides of the debate, and the very language we use carries values. Talking of 'evacuating the uterus' sounds very different from 'scraping out the baby'. Issues of the sanctity of life, competing rights and duties, women's control over their bodies and medical procedures and the provision and control of contraception and fertility are hotly debated.

Society's responses

Once abortion was unmentionable and almost unthinkable in polite society. Now it seems part of modern life; yet there is deep unease about the destruction of human life. The 'pro-choice' position argues that abortion is about women making choices about, and taking responsibility for, their own bodies. No-one can or should have any authority over the woman. If it is a choice between the life of the foetus and what the woman judges to be best for her and her other relationships or future, she must be free to choose abortion. Of course, she is also free to choose to continue the pregnancy. Society regards medicine's role as to protect women and to make abortion as safe as possible. The 'pro-life' camp stresses the sanctity of life from the moment of fertilization. Foetal life has as much value as any other human life, and because it is vulnerable it requires greater protection from society. This view also warns of the danger of abortion in terms of the psychological impact and possible future infertility. Some in this camp are conscious that there may be hard cases like rape and incest or where the life of the mother is genuinely at risk. Then they might allow abortion, but regard it as a lesser of two evils.

Society favours permitting abortion but does want some regulation to prevent abortion on frivolous grounds, for example where a pregnancy might spoil a holiday or a bikini line. Parliament has reduced the time period during which abortion is permissible to twenty-four weeks, although many in medicine would have liked it to be reduced even more. However, testing for certain abnormalities can be done only at a relatively late stage and so to prevent such births a later time was chosen.

As we hear more of multiple pregnancies and *in utero* (literally, 'in the womb') surgery, there is growing concern about the legal and moral status of the unborn child. While it seems extremely unlikely that society will return to a total ban on abortions, some restrictions seem to express deep concerns and attitudes about the control of fertility, contraception and the circumstances and effects of pregnancy.

Christian perspectives

Abortion is always a tragedy. But what ought to be addressed and prevented are the conditions that lead to the need for abortions in the first place. Few, if any, undertake abortion lightly. It usually stems from some kind of failure, and those involved need support and counselling.

God is the author and giver of life. He creates all human beings in his image. He is committed to humanity from the earliest stages of development. The psalmist and the prophets Isaiah and Jeremiah describe God's hand in creation and his call to them in the womb and his work on them there (Psalm 139:13–16; Isaiah 44:2–5; 49:1; Jeremiah 1:5). The principle of not killing innocent human life clearly rests on being made in the image of God (Genesis 9:5–6; Exodus 20:13).

The nearest the Bible gets to mentioning abortion is a reference to a miscarriage caused by violence against a pregnant woman (Exodus 21:22–23). The punishment is a fine rather than the death sentence which would have been required if the woman had died.

The New Testament describes the newly pregnant Mary visiting the very pregnant Elizabeth and how the unborn John the Baptist leapt in the womb in recognition of the coming saviour in the womb of Mary (Luke 1:41). While this does show foetal awareness, the identity stems from the knowledge we have of John the Baptist and Christ as we look backwards. It is less clear that it is possible to look prospectively from an embryo to the person yet unknown who will emerge.

Traditionally, the church stressed the idea that the soul entered the body. This led to difficulties about the exact moment this happened and even to the idea that men were ensouled before women. Rather than looking for a magic moment, it is clear that a human being is present from the earliest stages of conception. The issue is the value attached to life at different stages of development. We have seen in hospitals a growing sensitivity and better pastoral practice for those who have early miscarriages, acknowledging that there has been a genuine loss and bereavement and that human life has been extinguished. Talk of rights does not help order the conflicting priorities of rights nor define the responsibilities we have.

In the end, we have to ask if we believe it is ever justifiable to end human life. If it is, then are there circumstances when abortion, which is always evil for it involves killing, may be seen as a necessary but regrettable evil? That we need to justify abortion at all reveals that we really do believe that taking innocent life is wrong.

The church is in the business of bringing God's grace and forgiveness, but that requires recognition of evil and personal responsibility. It also requires supportive compassion for all those facing hard choices.

Something to think about

When does human life begin?

What value should we recognize at the different stages of human development?

How do you respond to the 'pro-choice' arguments?

How should you respond to women facing hard choices about abortions?

What are we to make of sperm and egg donors and surrogate mothers?

Background to the problem

When we meet people one of the inevitable questions is what family they have. For infertile couples this is very painful. One in five couples who want to have children are unable to, and that figure is on the increase. The problems are equally male and female infertility. Various techniques can help some individuals, but where there are fundamental problems with the sperm, eggs or womb, the option of donors and surrogacy arises.

Artificial insemination by donor uses sperm artificially to inseminate the woman. A woman may take drugs which make her produce many eggs, some of which can be donated to infertile women. Family, friends or women who are willing to sell their services may act as surrogate mothers carrying someone else's baby till birth.

These medical techniques create a whole host of problems for society. For example, what is a parent? What rights and responsibilities do donors have? Do children have the right to know their genetic origins? What is the role of payment in overcoming infertility?

Society's responses

Society is often totally oblivious and insensitive to the problems of the infertile. There can be a reaction of pity or a concern that there is something unnatural about medicine 'playing God' in such a deeply personal human matter. Given the high cost of such treatment, society is unwilling to bear the expense through the National Health Service, but does not seem to mind if people are willing to pay for it themselves.

As fertility work has developed, society, through the Human Fertilization and Embryology Authority, has brought fertility practices under close control and drawn important moral and social guidelines. Few would regard the donation of sperm as very significant. Masturbation and 'wet dreams' seem to waste sperm, so this puts sperm to some good use. Past, present or future sexual partners might have a different view of their husband donating sperm for someone else to have a child. Some have suggested that the use of a third party's sperm is tantamount to adultery, for even if there is no physical act of sexual intercourse, there is still the intrusion of life-giving material from another person.

Egg donation and surrogacy are much more intrusive. Super-ovulation and carrying someone else's child for nine months fundamentally affect a woman's life. Society's concern is to prevent exploitation of vulnerable women. This has led to the banning of surrogacy in return for money, although the payment of 'expenses' is permitted.

The law has tried to define what a parent is in these settings. It has ruled that the father of the child is the social father, the one who brings up the child, and not the sperm giver. The mother is the woman who carries the baby to birth, not the social or biological mother. These rulings were intended to encourage men to donate sperm and to discourage women from surrogacy as there were no further rights or responsibilities on the part of donors. This meant that, while couples were encouraged to tell the child the nature of their origins, there was no way for the child to trace his or her natural parent. This is under review, because adopted children do have that right and it seems unfair that IVF and AID children should be excluded.

Christian perspectives

There is a deep appreciation of the pain and distress caused by infertility and the effects this can have on relationships. The Bible has many examples of infertility, like Hannah and Sarah in the Old Testament. These women prayed that God would open their wombs, thus recognizing that God has the power to overcome infertility. Part of that overcoming now lies in the hands of medicine. Most Christians welcome medical techniques that enable married couples to have their own biological child. There are, however, some limits that most Christians would want to set.

The intrusion of a third party in the procreative relationship between a husband and a wife is not strictly adultery because there is no act of sexual intercourse. There is, however, an intrusion of life-giving material. The effects of such an intrusion in the long term for any relationship can be catastrophic. The idea that the husband or wife has produced a baby with someone else may undermine the marital relationship.

Christians must be concerned about all those involved in such settings. The child and his or her well-being should be the main concern. That the child knows the truth and is able to discover the biological parent seems a vital part of a truth-telling community and the developing of an individual's full sense of identity.

The donor also has to accept responsibility for what they have done and realize that that may involve being known and taking an active part in the child's growth and development. The problem with the law's definitions of parenthood is that it has created a major departure from our traditional understanding of what it means to be a mother or father. It also seems to enshrine the propriety of telling lies about our origins.

The Bible has an interesting example of one couple's attempt to overcome their problem of infertility. In Genesis we read of the promise of God to Abraham that he would be given children and they would become a blessing to all nations. Abraham believed it, but his wife Sarah did not, as she was past the age of normal child bearing. Sarah decided to take matters into her own hands and gave her maid, Hagar, to her husband to have a child. The result was a disaster. A child, Ishmael, was born, but it led to strife between Sarah and Abraham and between Sarah and Hagar. Hagar fled into the wilderness and was safeguarded by an angel, who prophesied that her son would live in constant dispute with others. Sarah did eventually have a son and God's promise was fulfilled. Some have even seen this story as the basis for the Arab–Israeli conflict, because Arabs claim Ishmael, and Jews claim Isaac, as their progenitor. Clearly, we have to be careful in taking matters into our own hands. The consequences for all concerned can be drastic.

We need to show understanding and sympathy for those who are infertile and unhappy. Modern medicine can provide many ways of having children, but there is still a moral responsibility to ask whether we should have children by any and every means and at all costs. The involvement of third parties is a recipe for disaster. Helping people come to terms with childlessness and learning to live with limits may be a better, though difficult, option.

Something to think about

How far should medical technology interfere with the natural process of child bearing?
Who is the parent where there are donated eggs or sperm or where a surrogate mother has been involved?
Do all children have the right to trace and know their biological parents?
How would you help a couple who were unhappy about being childless?

7
Death

Ending life and the end of life

Western society seems afraid of death and dying. The traditional rites of passage surrounding death have been undermined in a secular society, and we are not very good at dealing with those who are dying and with death itself. Dying has been removed from the setting of home and family into hospital. That provides a distance between the experience of death and the fact that it happens. Many middle-aged people have never seen a dead person or even lost someone close to them, like a parent. This lack of familiarity can create a fear of the unknown. Added to this is a fear of pain and suffering. In our pleasure-seeking society we will do almost anything to avoid physical and psychological pain.

At the same time, modern medicine can keep people alive artificially long after they would have died in the past. Many fear that medicine will turn from providing pain relief and comfort to prolonging dying. There is an almost inherent awareness that there is a time to let go, to let die and indeed to die. The very definition of death has shifted from the fact that breathing has stopped, to the heart has stopped, to brain death and brain-stem death. This makes people more anxious, wondering whether or not someone is really dead.

How we are to deal with the definition, experience and circumstances of our own death and the deaths of other people focuses on issues of euthanasia and assisted suicide. Deep spiritual, cultural and moral concerns lie at the heart of how we are to respond to questions of death and dying.

Is committing suicide wrong?

Background to the problem

Suicide is the deliberate taking of one's own life. Until the 1960s, it was a criminal offence in the UK. It was difficult to bring people to trial after an unsuccessful suicide, for the psychiatric hospital rather than the courtroom was deemed a more suitable place for the person. Some indeed suggest that there is a right to die. There is in fact now a *freedom* to kill oneself. There is no *right*, because this would imply that someone else had a responsibility to help.

The standard response used to be that suicide happened when 'the balance of the mind was disturbed'. Yet some people attempt suicide because they feel that they are a burden on others, that their life is not worth living because of suffering or a lack of meaning. These seem like rational grounds. There are multiple causes ranging from depression, physical illness to cowardice. Suicide is always a sign that something is wrong. It is often a cry for help.

There is a distinction between suicide and martyrdom. Suicide is self-centred, whereas martyrdom is for the sake of others or for a cause. The martyr does not wish to end life. If the same end could be achieved without dying, then that option would be taken. Death is the unavoidable consequence of performing an act of mercy, charity, piety or justice for the benefit of others.

Society's responses

Many people view life as a pursuit of pleasure and happiness. That means not just having all the good things successful people have, but avoiding pain and suffering. For the humanist or utilitarian, a life belongs to the individual. We are autonomous individuals, free to do whatever we want with our own bodies. If we are no longer happy or are facing an unpleasant, undignified and painful death, then we should be free to kill ourselves. The present is all there is, and if that is no longer pleasant, we are free to end it.

Existentialists believe that life is meaningless, and their question is why should we not commit suicide? In the face of dread and anxiety, suicide is a way out. Likewise, there is in some cultures a ritual form of suicide which happens when one has lost face, and embracing one's own death by one's own hand is a high form of virtue. In all these cases, human beings are the ones who determine whether or not a life is worth living. If it is not, there is a growing move to allow suicide and even to assist suicide.

Christian perspectives

In the creation account it is clear that human beings were created in the image of God and that God is the source and giver of life (Genesis 1–2). We are stewards of life and responsible for ourselves, each other and the rest of creation. We are not free to do whatever we want, not even with our own bodies, because we are accountable to God for all we do.

The Bible gives examples of suicides. Saul fell on his own sword after a defeat at the hands of the Philistines (1 Samuel 31:4). Ahithophel (2 Samuel 17:23) and Zimri (1 Kings 16:18) clearly destroyed themselves. Abimelech died at the hand of his armour-bearer rather than suffer the indignity of dying at the hand of a woman (Judges 9:54). Samson killed himself in taking revenge against the Philistines (Judges 16:28–30). In the New Testament, Judas Iscariot hanged himself after betraying Christ (Matthew 27:5). The Philippian jailer attempted to end his life when he feared his prisoners had escaped (Acts 16:27). The biblical picture is consistent. Suicide comes at the end of lives which were ruled by sin and immorality. When people live without reference to God, disaster results.

Suicide is a rebellion against God. It tries to take God's place and fails to recognize that life is a gift from God, bearing responsibilities.

Stewards are not free to return the gift whenever they feel like it. This does not mean that we should cling to this life by all means and at all costs. It is merely a temporal existence and has only full meaning in relationship with God. Death is not the end but a step in the movement from this life into the eternal dimension in the presence or absence of God.

This does not mean that suicide is an unforgivable sin. All sin is a falling short of God's standards and equally serious. God no more judges the last moment of life than all the other moments. God is a fair, just and loving God who will properly pass judgment. The idea that we should refuse people a Christian funeral because they committed suicide assumes that we can make decisions about God's perspective. This is something which should be left in the hands of God.

Christians need to address the issues and pressures that lead people to the brink of suicide. That there are alternatives to meaninglessness, loss of dignity, spiritual, psychological and physical pain and isolation should be the message and the practice of those who celebrate life in relationship with God.

Something to think about

What drives people to want to kill themselves?
How can we help them?
What is wrong with the suggestion that Jesus really committed suicide?
Do you think that God sends those who committed suicide to hell?

What is wrong with putting people out of their misery?

Background to the problem

We live in an age where pain and suffering are to be avoided at all costs. No-one should have to suffer, and if they are suffering and want to die, then they should be able to ask for assisted suicide or euthanasia (literally, 'an easy or gentle death', but it has come to mean 'mercy-killing'). Many people do not fear death itself but the pain involved in dying. We do not allow animals to suffer but put them out of their misery. How much more compassionate it is to relieve intolerable physical, mental and spiritual pain by helping people die, if that is what they want. There is a kindness which kills.

There is a distinction between active and passive euthanasia. The first is the direct causing of death by a third party, while the second is withholding particular treatment with the patient's consent. This withholding does not mean that the patient is not cared for or given pain relief. It means that the patient or doctor chooses not to begin a treatment that may not improve the medical condition. Even though doctors are trained to preserve life, they ought not to strive officiously to keep people alive if there is no hope of improvement.

Hospices not only create a context where people are able to come to terms with death and live until they die, they also provide a level of pain relief to enable people to cope with their distress. At times the level of pain relief may not only alleviate pain but also hasten death. This may not have been the intended effect, but shows the limit of medical science. It is very different from intentional killing. Frightening cases like that of Dr Harold Shipman, who killed over three hundred of his patients, show the danger of putting people out of their misery.

Society's responses

We have moved from medical paternalism to patient consumerism in the name of autonomy. Patients know best and are free to do whatever they want with their own bodies. In fact, however, autonomy is always limited in a community for the sake of protecting the individual from him or herself or to protect others.

Many fear the loss of dignity that can be part of growing old or of serious illness and would rather be dead than dependent on others for the basic necessities of feeding and toileting. This raises key questions about the basis of dignity. Is it more a matter of how individuals see themselves or how others treat them?

Compassion seems to indicate that helping people die is justifiable. The response to this is to ask whether in the name of compassion we are justified in going against the basic human taboo that killing innocent people is wrong. It is not clear that people are necessarily better off dead because we cannot wake them up afterwards and check that they are.

A House of Lords select committee examined the arguments for euthanasia and was unanimous in rejecting any move to legislate and allow euthanasia. Their concern was the danger of a progression from allowing euthanasia for those who are terminally ill and have a consistent wish to die to a situation where the elderly and vulnerable would be killed against their will. In Holland, where euthanasia is legal, up to one fifth of those undergoing euthanasia are killed without their own or their family's consent. It is difficult to see how a law could be drafted to guard against this kind of abuse.

There is also a widespread concern that any move that would alter the public's perception of doctors as life preservers to death controllers instead would undermine the trust and relationship between doctors and patients. Doctors are supposed to treat patients as individuals and do what is in each patient's best interests. He or she should not be given treatment because of pressure from the family, or the medical team or because others cannot stand to see the patient in pain. Patients sometimes claim they would be better off dead, but it is difficult to check that they are better off once they have been killed.

It is claimed that euthanasia is an act of compassion and that we would not let an animal suffer in the way we leave humans to, but it does not seem very compassionate to kill someone. Being compassionate does not mean doing whatever a person asks. Loving someone includes sometimes saying 'No'.

With the rise of the hospice movement has come increased pain-control technology. This movement had stressed the individuality of patients in their emotional, mental, physical and spiritual needs, and has made great strides in pain relief. So, patients can make decisions about how much pain relief they want and they should not have to die in pain. This reduces the need to kill people to put them out of their misery.

Christian perspectives

Christians should be in the forefront of seeking to alleviate pain. Medicine is a gift from God, and we should use it to help people. That is very different from killing people, for by doing so we usurp the place of God and break his commandments.

The creation account is clear in stressing that man and woman were made in the image of God (Genesis 1:27; 2:7). God breathed life into Adam and he became a living being. Life is a gift from God and death depends on God also. To attempt to control life or death without reference to God, and to believe that it is ours to do with as we please, is to rebel against God and seek to usurp his place. We are stewards of creation and answerable to God for what we do with it and with our lives. We are not autonomous beings but are ultimately responsible to God for the way we live and die and the choices we make.

The seriousness of taking human life is revealed in Genesis 9:6 where it says that, 'whoever sheds the blood of man, by man his blood will be shed', for such an act is not just against another human but destroys the image of the creator. The fifth commandment (Exodus 20:13) forbids killing innocent people. While it can be debated whether or not euthanasia is murder if the motives are out of compassion, it is clear that God takes seriously the sanctity of life and expects us to as well.

Suffering and pain are not to be avoided at all costs and by all means. The New Testament stresses many times that Christ endured suffering and trials but entrusted both life and death to God. He experienced the realities of suffering and could have asked to be returned to heaven, but instead chose to remain on earth and die on the cross. Without his suffering and death salvation would not have happened. Christ illustrates his power over death in raising Lazarus (John 11) and the son of the widow of Nain (Luke 7:11–15). Christ promises that whoever believes in him will not die, as he is the resurrection and the life (John 11:25–26). There are worse things than dying. Christ warns us not so much to fear those who kill the body, but those who kill the soul (Matthew 10:28).

Paul stresses the importance of Christ's resurrection and power over death and how it should affect our lives now (1 Thessalonians

5:10). He also stresses the role that suffering can have in maturing us as Christians, and that it is not to be avoided at all costs. We should expect persecution, and he writes from experience. Suffering produces perseverance, character and hope (Romans 5:3–4), and God is ultimately in control of our lives and deaths.

The song of Simeon (Luke 2:25–35) illustrates a proper attitude to death. Simeon had been promised that he would see the Messiah. That promise was fulfilled when Jesus was brought to the temple. Simeon prophesied what Christ would do and bring and then prayed that God would allow his servant to depart in peace. Christians should work to help others have a peaceful death, without killing them.

Something to think about

Why is our society so afraid of pain and suffering?

What limits should we set to autonomy and the idea that I am free to do whatever I want with my own body?

How can we help those who fear death and are in all kinds of pain and distress?

Are the consequences of euthanasia legislation the best kind of argument against it?

8
Politics and economics

Money, power and justice

It is supposed to be rude to talk about sex, money, politics or religion in polite company. Yet money makes the world go round. Whether we like it or not, money is a very important part of our lives. We spend a great deal of our time in trying to accumulate and then spend money. We have moved from a society of savers to one where consumerism is the natural order of the day. We also recognize the impact of international and national trade on ourselves and the rest of the world. The world economy is interconnected so that trade cycles and economic downturns in one country have a way of affecting the rest of the world. The behaviour of governments and multi-national organizations is public knowledge and raises public concern. Issues of environmental degradation and justice lie at the heart of our concern about trade and economic policies both within and outside our own nation.

This inevitably involves the political world. There is increasing disillusionment with the world of politics and politicians. Fewer people than ever even bother to vote, and no-one believes what politicians say or have much respect for what they do. Yet all that happens in the political world makes a fundamental difference to every aspect of our lives, especially in health, education, taxation and welfare. Whether we can afford *not* to be interested and involved in the political process is a crucial question. How we are to bring critical, moral reflection on political and economic issues is not just a Christian concern but part and parcel of what it means to be a citizen of our own particular nation and also of the world.

Why bother to vote?

Background to the problem

We live in a democracy, and that means that every citizen has the hard-won right to vote. Yet the turnout at many elections, especially at the local and European levels, is astonishingly poor. Governments are elected by a minority of the population. Part of this apathy may be a feeling that one vote does not make a very great difference, but there is also such a negative view of politics and politicians that people just cannot be bothered to vote one way or the other. Many feel that it is all cut and dried and so such and such a party or candidate will be elected regardless, so why bother? Such attitudes would have amazed those who longed for the freedom to vote and saw it as a crucial part of being a democratic community.

Society's responses

Society does not have a good word to say about politics, and views politicians as corrupt and only interested in themselves. Power corrupts, and politicians are caught up in the trappings of power. There is also the feeling that politics is just a game. Politicians howl at each other across the parliamentary chamber and then wander off to the bar to enjoy a drink together. It is seen as a game, remote from the genuine concerns of ordinary people. This stands in contrast to the excellent M.P.s who work exceedingly hard for the constituents they represent.

Part of the disillusionment and concern is that there are now so many levels of election ranging from the local to the national and European. With the rise of the Scottish and Welsh Assemblies, elections seem to be required at many different levels. At least, they only happen in the case of parliamentary elections every four years or so. This provides an opportunity to throw out the last lot and to try a new brand of party and politicians. In practice it seems that there is a decreasing difference between the various parties and a growing movement towards the centre of political life. Changes in the form of elections from the single direct vote to proportional representation have confused many people, though some would argue that this leads to increased participation in the democratic process.

Democracy depends on the active participation of each member. If we do not exercise our vote, it seems less than fair to complain about the kind of government and politicians we get. Yet there seems something deeply unsettling when a government can be elected with less than 50% of the vote.

Christian perspectives

God is intimately concerned with every aspect of human life and in particular with how we are ruled. The Old Testament law covered every area and aspect of life and the ordering of society. For the Israelites, theocracy (the rule of God) was the foundational form of government, but even that required some human expressions in terms of judges and leaders. All rule and rulers ultimately stem from, and are answerable to, God. He is the one who sets them in place (Proverbs 8:15–16). People in authority are meant to be careful about how they live and not to abuse their power. In telling judges how to judge in a righteous way, God indicates the need for appropriate behaviour, 'Do not pervert justice or show partiality. Do not accept a bribe' (Deuteronomy 16:19). Those who are in political authority are not simply judging and ruling on their own. 'Consider carefully what you do, because you are not judging for man but for the LORD, who is with you whenever you give a verdict. Now let the fear of the LORD be upon you. Judge carefully, for with the LORD our God there is no injustice or partiality or bribery' (2 Chronicles 19:6–7).

This is the same theme Paul presents in Romans 13, where he argues that all authority comes from God and that all rulers are answerable to God. They have been given a particular role by God, whether they recognize or acknowledge him at all. They are meant to restrain evil and to reinforce good.

Christians are summoned by Paul and Peter to pray for those in authority. It is a small step to see that God would expect Christians to exercise their voting power to ensure that men and women of good character are elected and policies which lead to the restraint of evil and the positive support of good are followed. If we are to act as salt and light, the use of the vote in a democracy is one way of fulfilling the role God expects of his people.

Something to think about

Why is the exercising of your vote important?
How can we raise the reputation and standing of politicians and the political process?
How does the Bible help me decide how to vote?
Should I vote for the individual or the party?

Which party should I support?

Background to the problem

British politics is based on party lines. Historically, different party groups have emerged sharing underlying philosophies and outlooks. In recent times those party groupings include not just Labour (currently New Labour) of the left, Conservative of the right and Liberal Democrat of the radical centre, but various nationalist parties ranging from the Scottish Nationalist Party to Plaid Cymru, Sinn Fein and the Ulster Unionists. These nationalist-based parties tend to have one key focus and may range widely on other issues from both left and right perspectives.

In elections we choose between the representatives of these parties. Often people vote for the party label rather than for the individual. Parties of the left, traditionally close to the trade unions, have supported high employment and the welfare state. Parties of the right have been committed to the free market, privatization, low taxation and low inflation. Currently, even these broad distinctions are increasingly blurred, and it is very difficult to define the exact differences between parties in terms of philosophies and policies. This makes voter choice increasingly difficult.

Society's responses

There is a wide disillusionment with politics. No-one believes what politicians say, and there is a widespread feeling that it does not really matter which party is in power, the results are much the same. There has been a shift towards the centre in politics, and there is a large measure of agreement about crucial elements such as the welfare state, education and a general approach to economic issues stressing low inflation, low taxation and maximum employment. Greater integration with Europe, particularly over a common currency, the Euro, does divide voters, but not along party lines. The voter is thus left with a choice of parties and candidates. The basis of the voting choice seems generally to be along party lines. Each party's election manifesto outlines what they stand for and contains specific promises about what will happen if they are elected to government.

Many cast their vote on the basis of what party will give them the best deal. Usually this is in terms of a better standard of living. Many voters are concerned about key issues of education, the health service and what is actually best for the nation as a whole. They are, in theory at least, willing to pay higher taxes for better public services.

There is often a personal following for a particular candidate. He or she may be well known or seen as a good constituency M.P. Occasionally M.P.'s behaviour causes such offence that the electorate rejects them. Neil Hamilton, a former Conservative government minister, was rejected for accepting bribes in favour of a 'Mr Clean' candidate, Martin Bell, who stood on the sole platform of anti-corruption.

Christian perspectives

Historically there has been a strand in Christianity which rejected any involvement in politics and refused to vote. This attitude stemmed from a desire for separation from the world and a refusal to be occupied with things that are transient. What was important was doing God's work and not being 'yoked [joined] together with unbelievers' (2 Corinthians 6:14). This attitude is less prevalent nowadays for it is clear that part of doing God's work is both to work for justice and mercy in every setting and to help those in authority restrain what is evil and encourage what is good (Romans 13:1–7). This means being involved in politics by, at the very least, following the political debate and exercising our democratic rights by voting. The Bible does not tell us who we should vote for nor should we expect that. Rather, the Bible is concerned that Christians seek that God's will be done on earth as it is in heaven (Matthew 6:10).

Voting is a serious business and requires careful thought, reflection and prayer. We are called to 'be as shrewd as snakes and as innocent as doves' (Matthew 10:16). We must assess the truthfulness and likelihood of the claims and promises made by different parties. In light of such an assessment we must weigh up the policies against the standards of what God seeks for communities and individuals. Christians believe that there are God-given standards of right and wrong, justice and mercy, which are required of those who exercise authority over us. In deciding how we cast our vote we should be judging politicians and parties against those standards. How will this party restrain what is evil and reinforce what is good (Romans 13)?

Christians more than others should not be casting their vote simply on selfish grounds but seeking the benefit of others, especially those who are vulnerable and needy in our society. God's concern for the vulnerable should be matched by our commitment to supporting them at every level. Loving others is the hallmark of exercising a Christian vote. Given that we have to judge between different parties and politicians we should be asking which party and individual is most likely to bring about policies and practices that are just, merciful and fair. Regardless of party label we are to pray for and honour those in authority (1 Peter 2:13–17).

Something to think about

How do you decide which party to support?
Is there an imperative for Christians to vote?
Why is there such disillusionment with the political process?
How can we work for justice and mercy?

Should the church be involved in politics?

Background to the problem

Great Britain has an established church, so the Anglican Church enjoys certain privileges and has responsibilities in the functioning of the state. It is involved in the coronation ceremony of the queen or king, Anglican bishops sit in the House of Lords and in society generally religious leaders are given wide and protected opportunities in broadcasting and the news media.

The fear and danger is that the church will either interfere in matters where it has no particular expertise and no right to put its nose in or that the church will compromise and fail to be the church. The problem is how the spiritual and temporal realms intersect and connect. It can seem unfair that one denomination has a privileged role and that some groups, like Roman Catholics, are forbidden from becoming or marrying the king or queen. Anglican clergy are forbidden to stand for parliament. The issue of disestablishment is raised not just by secular society but also from within the ranks of the church itself.

Society's responses

Society does not believe that the church should interfere in political matters. In a pluralistic, multi-faith society, it seems unfair that one group has a role denied to other faiths and denominations. Religious people are not in a majority, so again there is an element of unfair privilege. Many church leaders have no special expertise in political issues and should, therefore, stick to what they know.

Society thinks that the church should be the church and get on with looking after its own.

At the same time, however, when there are moments of national crisis, such as war, or tragedy, such as the death of Princess Diana, people look to the church to give a lead and to create a context for the expression of public concern and grief. Similarly, on moral issues like family, marriage, sexual behaviour and the whole gamut of social issues, people expect the church to speak out and to try to protect the vulnerable and to set a moral tone and give a moral lead. The problem is that society welcomes the church's intervention in areas like family breakdown but not on issues like abortion, stem cell research and anything that limits the freedom of individuals to pursue happiness in ways that do not harm anyone else.

Christian perspectives

For Christians it is odd to ask if the church should be involved in politics, for the Bible teaches that God is concerned with every aspect of human life. The story of the Old Testament is that of various forms of ruling, initially by God himself and then by judges and kings. In setting patterns for governance, God's concern was that justice was done and that all people were protected and able to flourish. In the idea of providence, God ultimately is in control.

> By me kings reign
>   and rulers make laws that are just;
> by me princes govern,
>   and all nobles who rule on earth.
>
> (Proverbs 8:15–16)

When he allowed the people of Israel to have a king, God not only warned them of the dangers of royal abuse but chose a suitable king and appointed prophets to remind the king of God's laws and will (1 Samuel 8–12; 2 Samuel 12:9–10; 1 Kings 16:30).

In the New Testament, Jesus teaches that we are to, 'Give to

Caesar what is Caesar's and to God what is God's' (Mark 12:17). Clearly, we all have obligations to the state and to God. Some, following Luther, have argued this implies that there are two separate kingdoms and thus two different realms and sets of standards. For Luther, Christ was lord of both kingdoms and so there can be no ultimate separation or difference in moral standards. Paul and Peter argue that we are to be subject to governing authorities for they are subject and answerable to God for the way they rule (Romans 13:1; 1 Peter 2:13).

Our UK government is largely based on Christian values. Christians have an opportunity and responsibility in parliament, schools and the media to proclaim the values of Christ. Christians have played crucial roles in changing the very fabric of society in the abolition of slavery and social welfare programmes. That does not mean, however, that the church should be in the business of compromise or should seek political power. Like the prophets of old, the church is to be prophetic, speaking out on behalf of the poor and vulnerable against injustice and reminding people of God's laws and the benefits and negative consequences of keeping or breaking those laws. Given the complexity of modern life and the difficulty of making wise political decisions, Christians should be encouraging godly people into political life and supporting them. Part of what it means to be salt and light is to ensure that the political processes do fulfil God's intention of restraining evil and reinforcing what is good.

Something to think about

Do we live in a Christian or post-Christian society?

What are the dangers in political involvement for the church and for Christians?

What are the dangers for society if Christians withdraw from politics?

How can we help restrain evil and reinforce what is good?

Do we have the right to inflict our views on other people?

Background to the problem

We live in a multi-cultural, multi-faith, pluralist world. Given the many different philosophies, faiths, moralities and outlooks, we have to live together. That will require tolerance and respect for other people's views. We must all have the maximum freedom to believe, express and practise whatever we want, as long as it does not harm anyone else. Tolerance, however, has to have some limits, and one of those is that no-one should force their views on others. Everyone is entitled to their view, even if we believe it is wrong.

Behind this lies a rejection of absolutes and an embracing of relativism, the view that there are no absolute truths or moralities, but what is true, good or bad varies from time to time, place to place and person to person. We have to admit that our knowledge and grasp of truth is partial, so we need to be realistic and humble about the limited nature of what we know. At best we can share our views, showing respect for other views and being open and willing to learn from them. We are free to express our views, but cannot pressurize others to accept our perspectives.

Society's responses

In a post-modern, relativistic world, everyone is entitled to his or her view, no matter how off-the-wall it seems. No particular view is better or worse than any other. It is considered arrogant to think you have the one and only truth and that everything else is wrong. Philosophy teaches us humility and that you cannot prove anything absolutely, so we must be cautious about our truth claims. Even science, which claims certainty, is really dealing with probabilities rather than absolutes. We are and should be free to pick and choose what helps and to reject the rest.

The heart of the western critical method is that everything must be open to scrutiny and doubt. If we cannot be sure, we cannot force others to accept our view. Religious faith is a matter of opinion based on belief rather than facts. One faith is as good as any other, so we must avoid indoctrination and inculcation. All of us, and especially children, must be free to learn and choose for ourselves. Parents and teachers must refrain from forcing their views on others. Respect, tolerance, humility and sceptical criticism are the values we need to embrace.

Christian perspectives

Christians must agree that no-one has the right to inflict his or her views on anyone else, and that it is wrong to force people to believe. It is impossible to produce genuine and real faith that way. However, it is perfectly proper for us to share our views with others, especially if we are convinced of the reliability, truth and importance of what we believe. If God has acted in the world throughout history, and most of all in Christ, then we should share that good news with others. Jesus constantly shared the good news of salvation with all he met, but he was careful to allow people the freedom to reject him and his message. The encounter with the rich young ruler in Luke 18:18–25 shows that even the king of glory allowed people to reject the way and embodiment of truth.

Christians must, however, reject the idea that all truth is relative and that all views are equally valid. That is not arrogance but common sense. Relativism is a dangerous, self-contradictory view. We do not and cannot live like that, and it is obvious that some ideas are far more sensible than others. That there is a variety of views does not mean that they are all of the same worth. Christians believe that in God is absolute truth, and in the physical and moral world God has provided a reliable base for living. In creation, the coming of Christ and Scripture we have an objective basis for right and wrong and how we should live.

When accused of inflicting our beliefs or morality on others, we should be clear that we are simply expressing God's standards. Of course, how this is done is crucial and requires sensitivity and appropriateness. In a democracy everyone is entitled to express a view as winsomely and persuasively as possible. Giving respect does not mean accepting everything another says and never disagreeing. One proper way of showing respect is in discussion and argument, making sure that both sides are free to accept or reject.

In the great commission given by Jesus to his disciples there is a clear command to preach and teach (Matthew 28:19–20). In the book of Acts, Peter claims the right to speak of what he had seen and heard (Acts 4:20). Christians have a responsibility to share the good news about Jesus, not least because of the awful consequences of not believing in Christ. That is no excuse, however, for assaulting people with our views and removing their freedom to accept and reject. Paul suggests that our speech should always be seasoned with salt so that we will know how to respond to each person (Colossians 4:6). We must be like Christ in offering what is true but always ensuring the freedom to accept or reject.

Something to think about

What is wrong with inflicting our views on others?
Does humility about truth mean that we should say nothing?
How has relativism affected our way of regarding truth?
How can we ensure that others are genuinely able to say 'No' to us and our views?

Are we what we earn?

Background to the problem

Sportsmen and women and film and pop stars make millions of pounds for doing what many regard as very little work. It is true that they entertain and bring pleasure to many, but do they deserve that much money for what they do? In contrast, most of us work long hours at what may be quite boring, routine jobs and are not paid a great deal. Whether we like it or not, there are great discrepancies in wages and salaries. Doctors are paid far more than those who sweep the streets. That seems understandable because of the long period of training and the high standard of education required and the life and death decisions which face many doctors.

While we may accept that there are salary differences, we may be less comfortable with the way that salary levels are often seen to define the worth and value of an individual. Prime ministers and their cabinet colleagues do not earn more than top businessmen and women. Our scale of values in terms of earnings and our perceptions of worth seem askew.

Society's responses

Everyone needs a living wage sufficient to support a family at a standard appropriate to the level of the national setting. People should be rewarded for the work they do, the effort they make, the years spent in education, preparation and training and the levels of responsibility they have to bear. There is concern that some people are paid too much and others too little. It is hard to know what can be done about excessive salaries and bonuses. The market and demands seem ready to carry that high level of salaries, even if it costs the shareholders and firms a great deal. How else can we attract and retain top quality people unless we pay the going rate? Increasingly, companies are presenting package deals to acquire senior staff, which include private health insurance and excellent pension arrangements. Some staff accept a lower salary level while in work because of the high level of security offered when they retire. Added to this is the job satisfaction and freedom offered in certain forms of employment. Academics are not well paid in comparison with other comparable levels of training, but they do enjoy great freedom and are able to work and do what interests them, and this creates personal and job satisfaction.

In dealing with low wages, governments have introduced the 'minimum wage'. This guarantees a level of payment for the poorest, no matter what kind of job or service they provide. Dishwashers and cleaners are often poorly paid, but now they are assured of the basic level of a living salary. What the level should be is debatable, but it is a step in ensuring that no-one takes advantage of those in employment.

Christian perspectives

Salary level does not define our worth. We are valuable because we are created in the image of God (Genesis 1:26). It is not what we do, or how much we earn, that gives us significance. Christians need to remind themselves and others that genuine worth does not consist in monetary rewards or the jobs we do. That does not mean that work does not matter. It is just not the most important thing in the world.

Proverbs 22:1 reminds us that 'a good name' should be chosen rather than riches, and Jesus constantly warned of the danger of riches blinding us to the really important things in life and eternity (Luke 12:13–34). Paul reminds those who make and have a lot of money that this carries responsibilities. They are not to be conceited or to fix their hope on the uncertainty of riches. They are to trust in God and to do good, to be rich in good works and to be generous and ready to share (1 Timothy 6:17–18).

Jesus commented that the worker deserves his wages (Luke 10:7). Paul reiterates this when he discusses elders (1 Timothy 5:17–18). Adequate and appropriate recompense for services rendered and work done is necessary and proper. There is a fine line to be drawn between giving incentives, recompensing for years of training and education and the special and sometimes dangerous nature of certain jobs over and against what is an immoral and unnecessary amount of money. Market rates for jobs must be matched by some kind of relative comparability. While jobs are not the same, there are similar levels of training, responsibility, expectations and function that should make it possible to produce a reasonable scale of salaries and benefits. Christians, recognizing the complexity and difficulty of such calculations, must be willing to help develop relevant scales. This is part of pursuing and seeking justice.

All this means that Christians should be in the business of working for fair and just wages for everyone. The Catholic Church has a long history of struggling for just wages and prices. Likewise, the Reformers were concerned that wages and prices were just. Often missionaries living and working in another country are paid at the level of those they minister to, rather than at what is often the much higher level of their home nation. This embodies a concern to ensure that there is a minimum and appropriate level which all should be able to maintain and that we have a mutual responsibility for each other. There have been striking examples of those who have given away or even refused salary increases. We need to remember that money and wages are not what define us, but rather it is our relationship with God.

Something to think about

Why do we pay pop singers and sports stars so much?
Why is the amount people earn so important?
How can we help people know their true worth in relationship to God?
How can we develop just wages for all?
How can we balance motivating and attracting people to jobs with comparable justice in wage and benefit levels?

What ought we to do about unemployment?

Background to the problem

Unemployment figures seem to be ever increasing, and governments struggle to bring down the numbers of those out of work. Mechanization and technological developments put jobs at risk as machines are able to do what human beings do but more quickly, effectively and cheaply. While initially technology may create jobs, in the longer term it leads to redundancy, unemployment or change of job. Where jobs are being created it seems to be in the service industry, and many fear the long-term consequences of this for the nation.

Work is necessary not just in order to live but to give a sense of worth and value. It may even define who we are and our significance. Sadly, many women when asked what they do for a living, reply, 'I am only a housewife.' Certainly our society seems to place more value on those who are in work than on those who are unemployed, and some jobs are rated more highly than others.

While many struggle to find a job, those in work complain that work is all-consuming. Those who work in the City are expected to put in long hours as a mark of their commitment to a job or company. Those who work hard are more and more concerned to play hard. The growth of the leisure industry shows the need that is felt for a release from the pressures of work. There are mounting levels of work-related illnesses such as stress and depression, and there is increasing evidence that many people are taking early retirement to escape from the 'rat race' and are moving to a simpler lifestyle and setting.

Society's responses

There are two distinct attitudes towards those who are unemployed. Some think that people are unemployed because they are lazy and do not try hard enough to get a job. In their view such people do not deserve a job or the social benefits to enable them to live without having a job. In contrast, cyclical economic patterns mean that certain kinds of jobs disappear and that many people will not have the appropriate skills to adapt to new job opportunities. They may also be unable or unwilling to move to where there might be jobs because of family and personal circumstances.

For those who lose their jobs there is often a sense of desolation, worthlessness and severe depression. It is extremely disheartening to be thrown onto the scrap heap and receive only rejection slips after many job applications. Society has to recognize that full employment is a myth and that there will always be those who are unemployed, and some of these may be unemployable. The question then is how our society is to help those people both by the benefit system and by enabling them, by retraining or job application help, to find new employment. Increasingly governments are in the business of job-creation schemes. Some even tie the receiving of benefits to genuine evidence of searching for work and a willingness to take a post if it is offered.

One of the key motives in pursuing higher education is the prospect of securing a better job at the end of it. The idea of a job for life, or even that there will be a guaranteed job at the end of a degree or training course, is a thing of the past.

In research about financial rewards and job satisfaction, it is interesting to note that the clergy are among the most poorly paid and yet show among the highest levels of job satisfaction. Work is not just for money and physical survival. It can give a sense of meaning and purpose to life and be a source of deep personal satisfaction. Unemployment can thus be all the more devastating in its impact with its loss of money, status and even a pattern of and structure for living.

Christian perspectives

God is a worker and he made human beings to work. He gave explicit commands about the work that was to be done. Humanity was to fill and subdue the earth, be fruitful and increase in number and name the animals (Genesis 1:28; 2:15, 20). All of this was to be done as stewards responsible to God. Even though the fall changed the conditions of work, work itself is not a curse but a blessing (Genesis 3:17–19).

When God gave the tribes of Israel the Promised Land, he intended them to work in developing what had been given (Leviticus 25:23). From the beginning God was concerned to protect the worker (Deuteronomy 24:14, 19; 25:4). God was also concerned to ensure that those who were unable to work, like the widows and children, were cared for (Deuteronomy 10:18; 15:7; 22:21). This concern is reiterated in the New Testament (James 2:2–4, 14–17; 1 John 3:17). In the early church this often took very practical forms (Acts 4:32; 6:1–4).

God himself showed a balance between work and rest from work. He commanded that same pattern for humanity (Exodus 20:9). We need to remember that those who are unemployed do not have rest or recreation. That balance has been taken from them.

If Christians believe that work was indeed part of God's creation plan for humankind, we must be in the business of job creation. Helping individuals and encouraging governments find and make job opportunities should be part of our care and support for those who are unemployed.

The Protestant work ethic showed how seriously Christians

regarded work following God's creation pattern. This was paralleled by the idea of vocation, where our work was seen as a calling of God and part of God's good will for the fulfilment and flourishing of human beings. Our own attitude towards work and to enabling others to find not just work but fulfilment in that work should reflect God's purposes for humanity.

Something to think about

Is work a curse or a blessing?
How should we regard those who have lost their jobs?
How can we help create jobs?
How can we regain an attitude of vocation towards work today?

Is it wrong to own property and shares?

Background to the problem

Property and shares are things we own, possess and have exclusive control over. Yet governments regulate how we may own, inherit and invest them and what we may do with something we regard as ours. Governments have used property and ownership as a door to voting rights, a means of gathering taxation and have made all this subject to legal limitations.

Ownership may be personal, familial or communal, including ownership by the state. Nationalization was a specific means whereby Labour governments in the past controlled utilities like water, power and transport. Now there is a reaction against such nationalization, and instead privatization is the flavour of the month, where individuals are encouraged to buy and own a stake in what was formerly owned by the state.

'Money, Money, Money. It's a rich man's world', sang Abba, and certainly money seems to make the world go round and open up all kinds of opportunities for those who have it. Contrary to this, those who do not have money, or very little of it, are denied access to all kinds of goods and services.

Society's responses

If money is so crucial, then you should accumulate as much as you want and need. Therein lies a problem because there may be a wide gap between what is needed as opposed to what we want. By and large, society regards the accumulation of wealth as an individual's private business. As long as the way we acquire and retain wealth is legitimate and does not break the law or harm people, then everything is justified. There is considerable pride in being able to make and keep money.

Yet society is also slightly prudish about money. Public displays of wealth are considered in poor taste. It is not bad in itself to have money, a nice house and all the trappings of an affluent lifestyle as long as it is not too ostentatious. Likewise, greed and the pursuit of money at the expense of other values like family, relationships and health are regarded as signs of moral failure and weakness.

On the one side, millions play the lottery each week in the hope of winning some vast sum, but on the other, when someone does win, they are often castigated for their vulgar spending and are expected to waste and ultimately lose their money. Winners and the wealthy are expected to be generous to their family and friends and to good causes. There seems a sense in which the ownership of wealth and property carries a responsibility to help the unfortunate and needy, almost to pay back for the good fortune.

Christian perspectives

The Bible tells us that 'the love of money is a root of all kinds of evil' (1 Timothy 6:10) and that if we seek first the kingdom of God, all the other things we need will be given to us (Matthew 6:33). There are no biblical rejections of property or share ownership, but there are many biblical concerns about the motives for and the pursuit of riches.

All property ultimately belongs to God (1 Chronicles 29:11, 14). God gave wealth to many of the Old Testament patriarchs like Abraham (Genesis 13:2) and Job (Job 1:1–3; 42:10–12). The commandments which forbid stealing and covetousness in Exodus

20:15, 17 establish the validity of ownership. Property rights were to be honoured. King Ahab is condemned for usurping Naboth's vineyard (1 Kings 21). It is clear that whatever was owned was seen as being held in trust for God. We are simply stewards of what God has given.

The New Testament continues that theme, especially in the parables of Jesus. We are to be good and wise stewards (Matthew 25:14–30; Luke 12:48). Wealth brings dangers and responsibilities. Jesus warns repeatedly about how riches can blind people to what is truly important (Mark 10:24; Luke 12:15, 32–34). We are to use wealth for the benefit of others (Matthew 25:31–46). Likewise, Paul warns of the dangers of greed (1 Timothy 6:6–10), and he reminds his readers that there is to be a balance between creating wealth and altruistic giving (1 Corinthians 16:2; Ephesians 4:28).

This sets the pattern for Christians as we reflect on how to invest our money. There is nothing wrong with money, but there can be a great deal wrong with the motivation for moneymaking and the way that we use the money we have and earn. All that we have comes from God, and we are responsible to him for the way that we create, use and abuse the wealth he has given. God calls us to show mercy on those who are in need. The example of the church in Macedonia in 2 Corinthians 8 reminds us that we are to respond to those in need and to share what we have so that all may have enough. There is a danger that we rely on wealth rather than God. There is also a danger that we spend too much time in wealth creation and neglect what is really important in life. Money is a means to an end rather than an end in itself. Accordingly, owning property or shares needs to be set in the context of our motives, aims and obedience to God's commands. Paul tells Timothy that we bring nothing into the world and will take nothing out (1 Timothy 6:7). Jesus encourages us not to lay up treasure on earth but to lay up treasure in heaven (Matthew 6:19–20; Luke 12:13–34).

Something to think about

What are our motives in owning property or shares?
Do we regard our wealth as God's or our own?

What difference does that make?
How can we help those who are in need?
How can we properly invest in property or shares?

9

Force and violence

Keeping the peace – home and away

Wars and rumours of wars still happen. There is always somewhere in the world where armed conflict is happening. Even after the atrocities of two world wars, world powers struggle to keep the peace. Issues of sovereignty and nationalism, in particular, still create tension, which leads to armed struggle. The United Nations has a difficult time in trying to resolve conflicts. Northern Ireland, the Middle East, many African nations and the Balkans are areas where violence seems endemic. The television news brings pictures from the front line, and we have become inured to scenes of death, destruction and violent acts and their effects. All of this lies under the shadow of nuclear, biological and chemical weapons and the threat they pose to the earth itself as well as to human beings. Deterrence or Mutually Assured Destruction is the global policy and Star Wars is the latest move in the game of peacekeeping and war avoiding.

The punishment system itself raises moral questions about the appropriate use of force and violence. Crime and criminals will always be with us, but what are we to do with them? How are we to balance the desire for retribution with deterring criminal activity, preventing harm to others and the genuine possibility of reform? Our penal system is in tension between all of these different and often mutually exclusive aims, and behind that debate lies another concerning the morality of capital punishment. How much force and violence can we allow the police and military forces to use in the pursuit and enforcement of justice?

How should we respond to violence in our society?

Background to the problem

All too frequently our television screens are filled with pictures of hooligans on the rampage. Violence seems a symptom of the breakdown of law and order, and there is a sense of frustration that expresses itself in violent acts. Parts of some inner cities have become 'no go' areas for the police because of the behaviour of alcohol-fuelled yobs. Increasingly, the elderly feel vulnerable to the threat of violence against them and their homes. It is not just robbery and theft that worry us; it is the mindless threat of violence without provocation. Road rage is becoming all too common. Parents are afraid to let their children play or walk home from school unattended in case they are abducted, raped, abused and even murdered. If we lived in the USA, we would be aware of the constant threat of accidental or intentional gun injuries, epitomized by the tragedy of the Columbine High School shooting. What happened at Dunblane and Hungerford in the UK reminds us that violence can strike at any time and in any place.

Society's responses

Those who are unemployed and socially deprived or live in areas where drug dealing is rife are more likely to turn to violence. Racial tension is also a factor and is related to poor education and work opportunities. If there is no hope of work or any improvement in personal and financial circumstances, violence is too easy an option. When there is nothing to lose, violence can give a semblance of power, even if it is misdirected. Historically, wars provided an outlet for violent behaviour. Now it seems to have been transferred to events on and off the sports field among players and spectators alike.

The past was no bed of roses where everyone was kind and caring. Various institutions and those in authority used violence in quasi-legitimate ways to threaten and control children, offenders and the 'lower' classes. Hanging and flogging were hardly kindly forms of punishment. With the end of corporal punishment in schools and many homes and the growing emphasis in the penal system on reform and rehabilitation, institutional violence seems to be decreasing. Our world seems more humane and less violent, though when violence does occur it seems shocking and difficult to cope with.

Christian perspectives

Christians should hardly be surprised that violence is always with us. Beginning with the Genesis story of Cain's murder of Abel (Genesis 4:8) the Bible is full of realistic accounts of the roots and fruits of violence. The example of Jesus stands in sharp contrast to the violent world of first-century Judea. The Roman legions and the Jewish Maccabean revolutionaries were not famous for turning the other cheek and their willingness to forgive and go the second mile. Yet that was the teaching and lived out example of Jesus in a very violent world (Matthew 5:38–45). His call was to reject violence and to respond to enemies by loving them. The force of love is greater than that of violence.

Yet there was an incident when Jesus himself used force to drive out the stall holders from the temple. They had changed the house of God from a place of prayer and healing to a den of thieves (Luke 19:45–46). Force for the sake of the protection of others seems to be permitted. Likewise, many regard the use of force in self-protection as legitimate.

Society and those in authority have a God-given responsibility to restrain evil and to reward good (Romans 13:1–7). The use of force is a proper means of achieving that goal. We may have to use force to restrain those who would harm others. Thus the police and the military may use force, but it needs to be controlled, appropriate and legitimate. That is one reason the 'just war' theory developed, in order to set limits to the institutional use of force and violence. It is only valid when all other means have been exhausted and only proportionate force is legitimate.

In a very real sense the resort to violence is a kind of admission of failure. Churchill famously said that it was 'better to jaw, jaw than war, war'. When we strike a child, then we are admitting that all other sanctions have failed and it seems that there is nothing else to be done. When the footballer kicks out at an opponent, it is often in frustration that the opponent is superior and cannot be stopped in any other way.

It is unlikely that Jesus would be willing to give up on people. His example and that of those like Gandhi and Martin Luther King who have tried to follow his path of non-violence and peacemaking are challenges to Christians to seek to be peacemakers in every setting (Matthew 5:9). This means creating patterns of restraint and helping individuals, groups and even nations learn peace. The prophets had a picture of what it would be like when violence was put to an end in the coming of the kingdom of God: swords would be beaten into ploughshares and spears into pruning hooks (Micah 4:3). Both Isaiah and the author of Revelation looked forward to the new heaven and new earth where violence would be a thing of the past and animals and humans would all live in harmony because they lived in the very presence of God. What will be true then can begin to happen today if we move from violence to a loving community where the need for violence disappears.

Something to think about

Where does violence come from?
Why do desperate people turn to violence against others?
How can we become peacemakers?
Is violence the only means of self-defence and the protection of others?
How far should we use force in order to discipline children and other people?

How can we justify having nuclear weapons?

Background to the problem

The traditional weapons of war have been overtaken by nuclear bombs which have transformed the possibilities of world conflict and its effects. In the nuclear bombing of Hiroshima and Nagasaki in 1945 we saw something of the long-term effects. Not only were those in the direct area killed, but also the land itself was contaminated and those in a wider area were affected with cancer, leukaemia and birth defects which have been passed on to future generations. The nuclear accident at Chernobyl reinforced our awareness of the dangers of nuclear power.

Since 1945 the major nations of the world have been in a nuclear arms race to build bigger, better and more destructive bombs. This has led to treaties to prevent nuclear proliferation and a concern about the dangers of nuclear weapons in the hands of dictators like Saddam Hussein or Colonel Gadaffi. The super powers have continued a policy of Mutually Assured Destruction (MAD) based on the philosophy of nuclear deterrence.

Society's responses

It is impossible to turn the clock back to a time before the invention of nuclear weapons. Everyone recognizes the awful long-term consequences for the world and humanity of using such weapons. No-one wants to use such weapons. The only debate is about how we are to prevent their use. Some argue that we must find ways of preventing the use of nuclear, and for that matter biological and chemical, weapons through international treaties. Others argue that a policy of deterrence is the safest way of making sure that nuclear weapons are never used. If you wish for peace, prepare for war. The threat of retaliation to any first strike use of nuclear weapons is meant to deter any would be aggressor. The price of using a nuclear weapon against one nation would be a massive retaliation from that nation or its allies. So by mutual threat there is a balance of peace. That threat must be seen as a serious intention or else the other side would not be deterred. This means that there must be a willingness to use nuclear weapons in retaliation against an aggressor. Not only is this seen as a necessary evil, it also involves a commitment to continuing to develop and maintain new, ever more destructive nuclear weapons to ensure that the other side does not gain an overwhelming advantage.

The incredible financial cost of such a strategy and the possibility of total destruction of the world and humanity terrify many to the point of seeking alternatives. Disarmament and other pacifist approaches seem the only alternative way to prevent mutual destruction.

Christian perspectives

Christians are opposed to the use of nuclear weapons but disagree over the morality of deterrence. Threatening violence is as bad as using violence. The intention to use seems to fall foul of Jesus' warnings about attitude being as harmful as actions (Matthew 5:21–22). It would be immoral to use nuclear weapons in a first strike, and to retaliate when your nation is assured of nuclear destruction looks like an act of revenge (Romans 12:17–21). Whether the command to turn the other cheek applies to nations and national self-defence is debated. Jesus' teaching is usually interpreted as a call to the individual in responding to personal harm done (Matthew 5:38–48). Helmut Thielicke offers the suggestion that you can tell the other side that you will not use your nuclear weapons as a first strike or in retaliation, but that you will keep them. If the other side is basically good and wants to avoid mutual destruction then together you can make peace and get rid of such weapons. If the other side is evil, they will imagine that having the weapons shows that, no matter what you say, you will, in fact, use them. Thus they will be deterred in spite of your honest rejection of the use of such weapons. He regards this as a moral way of deterrence which avoids threats, dishonesty and the use of nuclear weapons.

The Old Testament looks forward to a world of peace and harmony when God's rule is reinstated (Isaiah 2:4; 65:19–25;

Micah 4:3). Jesus calls his followers to be peacemakers, to love one's neighbours as oneself and to love one's enemies (Matthew 5:9, 44; 22:39). It is certainly hard to love people while 'nuking' them.

Christians should be working for peace between nations and discouraging not just warfare but the holding and using of potentially totally destructive weapons. That still leaves the problem of how we are to control those who have such weapons and are willing to use them. It is hard to see how the traditional Christian 'just war' theory can apply in a nuclear age, where there can be no protection of the innocent and the idea of only using proportional force is impossible. Rather, we need to follow Paul's call to pray for those in authority, 'I urge, then, first of all, that requests, prayers, intercession and thanksgiving be made for everyone – for kings and all those in authority, that we may live peaceful and quiet lives in all godliness and holiness' (1 Timothy 2:1–2).

Something to think about

Are there ever circumstances in which we should use nuclear weapons?
Is the only alternative to seek disarmament?
How might we control those who threaten evil and destruction?
Is the teaching of Jesus only for the individual and personal rather than the national level?

Are animal-rights protestors wrong?

Background to the problem

Scientists and their families are physically threatened. Laboratories are invaded. Funding sources are warned that they will be attacked. All of these are the actions of some protestors carried out in the name of animal rights. They want an end to animal experiments and regard violence as a legitimate means to achieving that end.

There is no doubt that there have been horrific examples of cruelty towards animals not just in laboratory settings but in homes and on farms, and that is an argument for ensuring that animals are properly treated wherever they are kept.

The activities of animal-rights protestors raise many questions about the nature and status of animals and their relationship with humanity. Is it right to hunt animals, to use them in medical and cosmetic research, even to eat them to sustain human life? Is it legitimate to kill animals for food but not for pleasure? Should we permit medical research but forbid cosmetic research on animals? Should we all become vegetarians and give up eating meat and fish?

Society's responses

Society has become more aware of the problems of how we treat animals. The Royal Society for the Prevention of Cruelty to Animals and other such charities have revealed the need for more humane care of animals. There are strict rules about how animals should be bred, looked after and slaughtered in farms, abattoirs and laboratories. A strict regulatory system and a team of inspectors enforce these. This, however, is not nearly enough to satisfy animal-rights protestors. Scientists argue that we need to use animals for medical experimentation because their physical structure will give us insight into new drugs, surgical techniques and treatments for horrific diseases. There is no substitute for animal experiments, for computer models will not provide the information needed to develop safe, successful treatments.

Underlying animal-rights protests is a rejection of what Peter Singer calls speciesism, a favouring of human beings over animals. He argues that we should reject such an ethic because it is based on creation rather than evolution, and instead of talking about the sanctity of human life we should concentrate on the capacity of all animals to feel pain and suffer. He says we need to realize that some animals are more important than embryos, mentally defective children and adults and people in conditions like persistent vegetative states. For many protestors this means that animals have rights and that humans ought to protect these animals and not experiment on them or use them for food or pleasure as in hunting. If scientists and researchers will not stop, then they must be made to stop, and violence is a legitimate weapon in the war against animal cruelty.

Christian perspectives

Part of the development of a proper concern about animals has come from a long tradition in Christianity stemming from Francis of Assisi and the early church fathers. No Christian should tolerate abuse of and cruelty to animals, but it is the reason for this stance which is important. In the beginning God created the animal kingdom, thus giving animals worth and value. The garden of Eden was a setting where humans and animals lived in harmony and humans were to name and care for animals (Genesis 1:26; 2:19). Because human beings are different they have a special role to play in relation to animals. Humans are made in the image of God and thus have a different nature and status. After the flood, animals were to be used for food (Genesis 9:3). God used Noah to protect animal life, but still animals were made to serve human needs. This is not a charter for abuse but a pattern of stewardship involving the protection and nurturing of animals.

On this basis, it is still important to evaluate the animal-rights claims. If humans are created in the image of God and different from animals, then animals do not have rights in the ways society regards humans as having rights. That does not mean that we have no responsibilities to animals, but that responsibilities to human beings come first. In a fire, saving a person would be more important than saving a dog or cat, not because animals are not important but because human beings are more important.

This is both natural and common sense. While many deeply appreciate having a pet and the joy that brings, there is a fundamental qualitative distinction between humans and animals. We need to be careful not to imagine that animals feel exactly what human beings feel. (When your dog seems to be smiling at you it is usually just a case of excess wind.) The blurring of that distinction is seen in Singer's proposal that in certain circumstances abortion, infanticide and the destruction of those with dementia and Parkinson's disease is justified, if this will help alleviate the burden on society.

Christians can never condone the use of terror tactics and violence against those who are seeking to bring health and healing to others. That makes it seem that animals are more important than human life and well-being. Other cultures, where animals are regarded as there for the benefit of human beings, are amazed at the British fascination with pets and animals. We have a responsibility for the care and welfare of animals, but that must take second place to our responsibility to humankind.

Something to think about

Are there key differences between human beings and animals?
What responsibilities do we have for animals?
Why do we think that scientific, medical research should continue?
How can we ensure animal welfare?
Do you think that animals have rights?

Should Christians ever go to war?

Background to the problem

War still ravages many nations and people. The effects of war on communities are very great. All over the world the weapons industry creates wealth for individuals and countries. Politicians try to avoid war, and when conflicts do arise they try to find some peaceful agreement. War is clearly an evil to be avoided, but not necessarily at all costs.

The idea of a just war brings a measure of control into war situations. This seems contradictory, for in war it seems that anything goes. Yet various conventions have been drafted, for example the Geneva Convention which sets out how prisoners of war are to be treated. The International Court of Justice seeks to bring to justice those who have committed war crimes, specifically 'crimes against humanity'. While we recognize that war is inevitable, we do try to set some kind of boundaries around its conduct.

Society's responses

Society tends to view religion as often responsible for war. The Crusades and situations like Northern Ireland are examples of religious divides leading to warfare. Yet society has also embraced the religious ideas of setting limits to war contained in the 'just war' theory. Some argue that the advent of nuclear and biological weapons of mass destruction has made this concept obsolete, but in the Falklands conflict and the Gulf War politicians were quick to appeal to the idea of a just war to defend their actions.

Behind the idea of a just war was the intention to set limits to the atrocities of war and to give some guidelines for its conduct. War must be a last resort, waged by a legitimate authority and involve a formal declaration of war so that it is clear who is and is not involved. The aim of military action must be a just and lasting peace, and the harm done in the war must be less than the harm that would have been done if no war had been waged. There must also be specific attempts to limit the harm done to non-combatants and to ensure the use of proportionate force. On the world stage, leaders defend their military actions in relation to these kinds of arguments.

Of course, the real aim is to make peace and avoid or end warfare. This inevitably involves a degree of compromise. The example of the Second World War shows that there are some atrocities and evils which must not be tolerated but resisted by force if necessary. The protection of others and self-defence are usually the grounds claimed to justify war.

Christian perspectives

In the Old Testament, war was a regular occurrence. Wars commanded by God are often called 'holy wars' because of the divine command and purpose involved. War was to defeat enemies (Deuteronomy 7:2, 16), to seek revenge against nations (Judges 20:8), to defend allies (Joshua 10:6–11) and to bring liberation from oppression (Judges 6 – 8). Many of the great heroes of the Old Testament, like David, Joshua, Caleb and Gideon, were successful generals, though it is interesting that David was not allowed to build the temple because of his warfare.

Jesus foretold that there would be wars and rumours of wars (Mark 13:7). His commands to love our enemies (Matthew 5:44), to turn the other cheek (Matthew 5:39) and to offer forgiveness (Mark 11:25) seem at odds with the idea of war and have led to the pacifist movement, which rejects the use of force and seeks creative ways of bringing peace.

Jesus himself, however, used force to drive out the money changers (Mark 11:15), and he never commanded soldiers to give up their occupation. He commanded that his followers render to Caesar the appropriate duties and obligations as long as these did not interfere with their responsibilities to God (Mark 12:15). Paul, following the example of Jesus, often referred to the Christian life as a spiritual battle for which we need to be properly equipped (Ephesians 6:10–18).

Whether or not a Christian can be involved in war depends on the individual's conscience before God and how the Bible is understood. Is the teaching of Jesus about turning the other cheek meant only as a response for personal insult and injury? Is it appropriate for us to forgive on behalf of others for wrong done against them? Surely, we are expected to defend others and protect the innocent and vulnerable? That indeed is the role of those in power and authority as outlined in Romans 13. Dietrich Bonhoeffer, a leading German theologian, was so appalled by the atrocities and policies of Hitler that he plotted to kill him. He was captured, tried for treason and executed. Bonhoeffer's theological perspective was that he was guilty of sin, but he could not stand by and do nothing. Even if it was the lesser of two evils, it was still an evil to kill another human being. Bonhoeffer said that he was willing to become sinful, not expecting forgiveness but throwing himself on the mercy of God. No Christian should enter into a war lightly or underestimate the seriousness of the consequences of their action or inaction.

Jesus said, 'Blessed are the peacemakers, for they will be called sons of God' (Matthew 5:9). Christians, whether they choose to fight or not, should be in the forefront of all attempts to make a just and lasting peace.

Something to think about

How are we to reconcile the Old Testament view of war with that of Jesus?
Are the commands to forgive and turn the other cheek only for personal wrongs done?
Is it possible to control war by the 'just war' criteria?
How can we be involved in making and keeping peace?

Why do we punish?

Background to the problem

If you visit the Old Bailey you will see a statue representing Justice. She has in one hand the scales of justice and in the other a sword. The scales imply that a crime committed imbalances the scales. To put that right you place a punishment in the other scale and so the balance in society is restored. The sword indicates that the infliction of pain is the role of justice. She is blindfolded to show that justice is impartial for all. Society has to protect its members and itself. When wrong is done and the law is broken, society punishes to show the seriousness of what has happened, to try to prevent it happening again and to try to help the offender recover and the victim draw a line under what has happened. Punishment is the authorized infliction of pain or deprivation on someone who has committed a crime. It is authorized because this is not revenge but the application of a legal system wherein the crime and the punishment is defined. The guilty person suffers because of what they did, their intention to do it and the breaking of the law which is involved. The punishment is for the crime rather than for their background, experience or personality. The actual role of punishment is hotly debated in society.

Society's responses

When the law is broken and a crime committed, people feel someone should pay for it. Retribution is deep in our hearts and minds. Some kind of reparation, compensation or restoration of the status quo is important. This rests on the biblical principle of 'eye for eye and tooth for tooth' (Exodus 21:24; Deuteronomy 19:24). The problem is how to make the punishment fit the crime.

Punishment is also meant to deter the individual or others from committing the same kind of crime again. Judges often talk of making an example of someone. Capital punishment is the area where deterrence is most disputed. It is far from clear that deterrence actually works, especially when a crime is committed in the heat of the moment or when the risks of being caught and found guilty are carefully calculated.

Prevention and protection in terms of punishment usually mean imprisonment. Locking people away prevents them from reoffending for some time. Sadly, it seems that prison often does not change people in the longer term, and there is an high level of repeat offending. Indeed some critics regard prisons and young offenders' institutions as schools of crime.

Reform is the other aim in dealing with offenders. Probation or imprisonment gives an opportunity to work with criminals to try to help them live as law keepers rather than lawbreakers.

There is a relatively recent move in penal theory called restorative justice which seeks to restore the relationships between the victim of the crime and the offender. This is often a hazardous matter, but is an interesting way of trying to restore the balance disturbed by the crime.

Unfortunately our penal system tries to do all of these things at the same time. While we recognize that home, school, unemployment, poverty, community and personality all play a part in the likelihood of someone breaking the law, we still hold that person responsible for what he or she has done. Society has to have rules, and when these are broken society must treat such violations seriously and punish offenders.

Christian perspectives

Punishment and reward are two sides of the same coin. The way that we live, the choices we make and what we do carry inevitable consequences. If we make good choices and live properly, we will flourish. If we make bad choices and do evil, we will suffer. This is part of what it means to live in a moral universe, where all we do makes a difference to us and to others. When Adam and Eve sinned and broke God's law (Genesis 3), there was an inevitable consequence. They were ejected from the garden paradise and their relationships with each other, with nature and with God were fundamentally affected. This theme is reinforced in the book of Deuteronomy where keeping or breaking God's law carries consequences of blessings or cursing (Deuteronomy 12:28). This was necessary to preserve that society and protect individuals. The point of punishment for breaking the law was to warn others of the seriousness of such behaviour, to punish the lawbreaker and to try to restore him or her.

Often in the Old Testament the threat of punishment is used as a warning to prevent something happening and therefore to reform the way of life. The Old Testament has many examples of what we regard as extreme punishment (e.g. Micah 2:1–4). This shows the seriousness of sin and crime.

Punishment for crime is not at odds with the stress on forgiveness that should mark the Christian. We are told to turn the other cheek and to forgive 'seventy-seven times' (Matthew 5:39; 18:21–22). This is a call for an individual to forgive those who sin against him or her. Jesus embodied this principle in asking God to forgive even those who crucified him (Luke 23:34). This is quite different from the role of the state, protecting its members. Personal forgiveness in no way undermines the authority of the state to inflict punishment (Romans 13:1–7).

Jesus, as the Son of God, was able to forgive sin, as in the case of the woman caught in adultery (John 8:5–11). Nevertheless, sin is taken so seriously that Christ died for the sins of others (Romans 5:8). Christians are not to indulge in vengeance, recognizing that punishment belongs ultimately to God (Romans 12:19), but that does not mean Christians are careless about punishment.

Proper punishment begins in the home. The book of Proverbs outlines appropriate discipline as a way of educating and helping children to recognize the difference between right and wrong living (Proverbs 13:1; 19:18; 22:6; 23:13). This is no charter for exploitation or abuse, but a proper and sober responsibility for parents. As citizens, we have a responsibility to help preserve the law and to make the law fulfil its goal of reform, restoration and reconciliation.

Something to think about

Why do we punish people?
How do we view the punishment God meted out in the Old Testament?
Does the command to forgive others mean that we must accept and allow all kinds of wrongdoing?
How can we help to restore those guilty of crimes?

Should we have capital punishment?

Background to the problem

There has been a growing rejection of capital punishment in Europe, but some parts of the United States and China retain such punishment. Capital punishment is the taking of a person's life by the state in response to a serious crime, such as murder. It is not revenge, but justice. Some crimes are so serious and awful that the only appropriate response must be the taking of life. The value and worth of a life is shown by the requirement of a life for a life. The general public seems to support capital punishment, though legislators are increasingly concerned about the barbarity of such measures and of the possibility of miscarriages of justice, leading to the execution of innocent people. Such public support points to a deeply held desire for retribution and feeling that the punishment should fit the crime. Likewise, there is a sense that some would be deterred by the threat of capital punishment. Some families are very vocal in demanding the death penalty as the only appropriate sentence for the murder of a loved one, and tabloid newspapers often whip up support for such a view.

Society's responses

Societies which favour capital punishment argue that retribution and deterrence are the key bases. Retribution means a life for a life. It holds all of us responsible for our actions. If we take a life, we must forfeit our own life. The inflicting of the death penalty is the only way of guaranteeing that this person will not commit a crime again. It restores the balance of justice in society, and it allows families to move on from the murder of a loved one with a sense that justice has been done.

At the same time, deterrence means that people will be hesitant to commit any crime which carries the death penalty. Murder rates should fall and people would be safer because of the capital punishment.

Those opposed to capital punishment are concerned about the barbarity of such a 'cruel and unnatural' punishment. Civilized societies ought not to stoop to the level of those who have committed murder by permitting institutionlized murder. Life or long-term imprisonment can achieve prevention. Deterrence does not work, it is claimed, because there is not a lower murder rate in countries with the death penalty than in those without it. Deterrence only works if people are likely to be caught and punished and certainly does not seem relevant in cases of crimes of passion. There have been too many miscarriages of justice for juries or legislators to be comfortable in applying a death sentence.

On either side of the debate is a recognition that we do not know what to do with people who commit heinous and outrageous crimes. If rehabilitation is unlikely and prevention necessary, what is a society to do to protect its members?

Christian perspectives

Exodus 20:13 and Genesis 9:6 set the context for any Christian discussion of capital punishment in proclaiming that murder is wrong and that a life is required for a life because people are made in the image of God. One of the Ten Commandments condemns the taking of innocent life (Exodus 20:13). In the rest of the Old

Testament punishment threatened or inflicted by God is often in order to restore people to a proper relationship with him. Jesus came not just to bear the punishment deserved by humanity but to show and enact a new covenant. At the heart of the new covenant is the realization that anger and lust are as bad as murder and adultery (Matthew 5:21–22, 27–30), and that we are to forgive and show love for those who do us harm (Matthew 5:38-42; Luke 6:27).

Love and forgiveness do not fit easily with capital punishment. In his response to the woman caught in adultery Jesus replaced retribution with reconciliation (John 8:1–11). Many argue that the death of Christ ended the role of retribution and ushered in a new covenant. Jesus certainly warned of the danger of eternal punishment, but this seems to be a call to repentance based on a desire that none should perish.

Paul affirms the validity of civil authority and its right to punish in Romans 13. He also reminds us that we are not to wreak vengeance on others but to leave that in the hands of God (Romans 12:19–20).

It is not easy to affirm a punishment which removes the possibility of repentance, rehabilitation, forgiveness and mercy. At the same time, we are left with how we are to interpret the Old Testament in light of the teaching of Jesus and a concern for all those affected by serious crime that takes life and for those who commit such crime. Making life imprisonment a genuine punishment, yet allowing room for renewal and change is not easy to balance with the desire for justice.

Something to think about

When, if ever, do you believe that capital punishment is justifiable? What might be put in its place?

How are we to understand and apply the Old Testament teaching on capital punishment?

How are we to apply the teaching of Jesus when the crime is committed against someone else rather than ourselves?

10
The media

Watching and watched – voyeur or spectator?

Marshal MacLuhan suggested that the medium is the message. We certainly live in a media saturated world. The print and broadcast media provide us with the information and entertainment we need to make sense and live well in the twenty-first century. The problem is that we often have 'narrow casting' rather than broadcasting. Editors and producers select what news we read. They decide what is newsworthy and what angle or 'spin' to give certain stories. They decide who will present the stories and what expert or pundit will be invited to comment. The news we have is not the whole news but a refined selection, filtered through many layers and agendas. This raises key questions about truth, transparency and bias.

Pictures are extremely powerful. A picture is worth a thousand words and the pictures from television, the internet, films and video batter our consciousness in our homes or in the cinema. It is not easy to wipe out or forget such pictures, and they are not neutral but carry values and attitudes. Advertisers realize the power of the visual and use it with suitable sound effects and music, so we find ourselves humming a familiar tune and buying a recognizable product when our visual stimuli are captured.

What is true in the world of advertising carries over into the world of entertainment. The danger is that we become what we watch. There is growing concern about the effect of explicit sexual and violent material on our children and us. We are all horrified that the murderers of Jamie Bulger had been watching a violent video and seem to have re-enacted some of the scenes while taking a young innocent life. Thus we need to consider what kinds of limits there should be on what we watch and are allowed to watch. Key issues of personal and social freedom collide with protection of the vulnerable.

The way in which women are portrayed in the media and the impact of such portrayals on us all again raises questions of how explicitly violent and sexual matters should be displayed. The media is an important part of modern life, but how should it be controlled and regulated?

Should advertising be more carefully controlled?

Background to the problem

Images, punch lines and even stories are used by advertisers to sell their products. The pictures of a child running down a lane in Vietnam covered in napalm or of a Chinese student in Tiananmen Square show the power of the visual. Advertisers trade on that power and seek to match some clever selling gambit with an awareness of their particular product. They want to sell and for us to buy. They are in a competition against other producers and are seeking greater market share by persuading us that we need some particular product. So the latest after-shave will have women swooning and then flocking to follow the man who wears it. A scantily clad woman sitting in a car carries the message that if you buy that kind of car then you will be attractive to members of the opposite sex.

The more competitive business becomes, the more creative and outrageous advertising can become. Benetton, for example, produced a series of adverts using images of blood and violence which were both offensive and verging on the blasphemous. We want freedom to advertise, but should there be limits?

Society's responses

There is a balance between allowing free commerce and protecting the vulnerable. While society is more tolerant and permissive, it also realizes that advertising can be harmful and 'economical with the truth'. The portrayal of women in sexually provocative poses to sell products which have no relation to sexual matters not only degrades women, but raises false hopes, expectations and perceptions. There is a tension between advertising underwear and using pictures and positions which imply that wearing that underwear will inevitably lead to sexual success.

The use of animals and children in advertising is also highly dubious, both in the portrayal of the children and animals and in what they are made to do to sell a product. Children's toys are only advertised at certain times. There is a recognition that the power of advertising will actually create a demand rather than offer choice. Advertisers debate the balance between the giving of information to allow genuine choice and the creating of a need when one was not there before. There are also concerns about the truth of advertising. If a particular beer refreshes the parts other beers don't reach, what on earth does that mean and how could it be proved one way or the other? The Advertising Standards Authority is the recipient of complaints about the truthfulness and decency of what is advertised. They will censure and fine those who cross the line and use offensive and misleading advertising. Some respond by saying that we all know that these are just adverts and are not duped by their claims. People are not stupid and they realize that hype and exaggeration are part of the advertising game. This may be highly optimistic in that it makes no allowance for the psychological and subliminal impact of advertising. When we go into a grocery store we are not always aware that the goods have been carefully placed to create certain positive responses and to encourage us to buy more.

Increasingly, cigarette advertising is tightly controlled even in the context of motor racing which is sponsored by tobacco companies. You are not permitted to place cigarette adverts near schools, and television cigarette advertising is severely limited and controlled. The freedom to advertise is not without limits.

Christian perspectives

The Old Testament laws were given to protect society from disease and social calamity. Likewise our advertising laws seek to protect the vulnerable. In an age when credit is all too easily available, advertising may encourage people to buy more than they can really afford and so create a cycle of debt. People also need to be protected from having unwanted pictures forced on them. They need to know that the information advertisers give is reliable and trustworthy. There must be a distinction between lying and telling the truth even in adverts. Ephesians 5:15 warns us that we need to look carefully at how we live. It is all too easy to become attracted to the good things of this world which pass away (1 John 2:15–17). Greed and acquisitiveness are to be rejected. Peter warns us that the devil is on the prowl seeking someone to devour (1 Peter 5:8). We are all vulnerable to temptation and need to guard against it. That is all the more difficult when advertising insinuates and cajoles in subtle ways.

Jesus was scathing about what happens to those who offend the vulnerable, particularly little children (Mark 9:42). We are our brother's and sister's keepers and so must be careful not to use a proper freedom in Christ to cause harm to others (Romans 8:9). Such concern for others should lead Christians to support careful and thoughtful regulation of advertising. It will require the highest standards of truth and decency and it will reject the depiction of women, children and animals in sexual, violent or degrading contexts. It will encourage proper creativity but prevent the abuse of the trust and freedom that advertisers enjoy. It will also draw attention to the motivating and driving force of money in the business and advertising worlds and the need to ensure that truth, freedom of choice, reliable information and appropriate presentation of products is the norm and not the exception.

Something to think about

Do adverts influence us?
How can we judge the truth of advertising claims?

What is wrong with certain depictions of women, children and animals?
Should we control advertisers and advertising more rigidly?

Is there too much invasion of privacy in the media?

Background to the problem

Newspapers and magazines are in the business of increasing their sales and thus making a profit. Sex, violence and money scandals sell copies. The public loves to hear the dirt being dished on the rich and famous. The royal family, politicians and sport, film and pop stars are all considered legitimate targets for press interest. If there is a hint of any kind of misconduct then the public wants to know about it. The problem is how to distinguish between a legitimate and necessary right to know what has happened and what kind of person we are dealing with and situations where the press are pursuing, photographing or even setting people up to entrap them. Princess Diana was photographed by a hidden camera while exercising in a private gym. The Countess of Wessex was taped making disparaging remarks about other members of the royal family and leading politicians in what she had been led to believe was a business meeting. Even ordinary people suffer from press intrusion as a microphone is thrust in their face after some personal tragedy and they are asked to make a comment.

Society's responses

Everyone is entitled to privacy. Part of the dignity of being human is that what is personal and intimate is not for public consumption. When doctors swear the Hippocratic Oath they promise not to divulge information about their patients. There is widespread concern about the practice of 'outing' people in public life and revealing that they are homosexual. Many regard such information as properly personal and in no way the business of anyone else.

It is, however, important to distinguish between what is in the public interest and what interests the public. We may all be fascinated by even the grossest sexual peccadilloes of other people, but it is doubtful if we need to know such information. The question is whether how someone lives and acts in private in any way affects how well or badly they are able to do their job. As long as they are not cheating their employer or the public, then whatever they do in private is all right. Others will feel that we have a right to know what kind of person we elect and whether or not they are honest. Society hates hypocrisy and when someone sets himself or herself up as a public figure then they need to realize that they will be open to public scrutiny. If they are liars or cheats and try to mislead and pretend to be other than they actually are, then they are fair game. Libel and slander are the legal remedies pursued to protect against lies told in the media.

Society is concerned to protect those who are simply private individuals and have no public role or experience of coping with the demands of public life. Children too are to be protected from press intrusion until they are able to choose for themselves.

Christian perspectives

Jesus showed that there should be no gap between what we say and do and who we are. He was integrity personified and is the model we should seek to follow. That is why we are called to imitate Christ (Ephesians 5:1). Those who exercise leadership in the church are meant to uphold high moral standards (1 Timothy 3:1–13). All Christians are expected to live lives of honour and to try to be above reproach (Colossians 3:12–17).

Those who enter public life are, quite rightly, subject to public scrutiny. The public has a right to know what kind of person they have elected or trust to represent them in some way. Issues of truth, honesty, integrity and straightforwardness are fundamental to public confidence. That does not mean, however, that we are entitled to know everything about everyone. Jesus was bitterly critical of the hypocrisy of the Pharisees and Scribes (Matthew 23:13; Luke 6:42). Those who pretend do harm to themselves and others.

When assessing whether or not press interest is an invasion of privacy, it will be proper to ask what the motive is for this pursuit. As we expect people in public life to be accountable, so the press must also be accountable. There must be particular concern about those who are vulnerable. When a tragedy strikes or a disaster happens, it is degrading and embarrassing when over-zealous reporters intrude into the grief of relatives and take advantage of people at a vulnerable time. Children too need to be allowed to grow up and to make mistakes without being hounded by the press.

It is sadly no surprise that some stars and leading figures are driven into alcohol and drug dependency, because the price of fame is a lack of freedom and balance in one's personal life.

Much of what passes for news is in fact nothing less than gossip. James warns of the danger of the tongue (James 3:1–12). Proverbs 26:22 picturesquely states, 'The words of a gossip are like choice morsels; they go down to a man's inmost parts.' What we say and write about people and the pictures we take of them may have a lasting effect, not just on them and their futures, but on us as the readers, listeners and viewers. This is why Paul reminds us in Philippians 4:8 that we should concentrate on wholesome, constructive things.

The danger of the invasion of privacy reminds us why people are important and that their personal life, space and being ought not to be harmed. It also shows the cost of engaging in public life and the need for legal and practical protection for the vulnerable from inappropriate intrusion.

Something to think about

Why are we so fascinated by the sexual details of the rich and famous?

How may we distinguish between the public interest and what interests the public?

Do you believe that there is a clear line between the private and the public life?

How may we protect the vulnerable from press intrusion?

Is retreat to the libel and slander laws too late to be really helpful?

How can we control pornography?

Background to the problem

What is shown on our television and film screens and available in newsagents is much more sexually explicit than it was just a few years ago. The arrival of the internet with its chat rooms, and access to the worldwide web means that all of us have the possibility of discovering material that is regarded as pornographic. It is not always easy to define what is pornographic. Some suggest you know it when you see it, but usually it is material that is not just sexually explicit but also offensive. It has a tendency to 'deprave and corrupt' and lacks any serious literary or artistic merit. Pornography assaults the sensibilities of the viewer. It has moved from the top shelves in shops, carefully sealed in cellophane, to being easily accessible. Films, videos, the internet and even television carry sexually explicit material which many find offensive and certainly do not wish their children to be exposed to. At worst, pornography degrades and exploits not only women but also children. It takes advantage of the vulnerable both in terms of the sexually inadequate and those who are unable to refuse to take part.

Society's responses

In the name of freedom of expression and artistic licence, many regard pornography as much ado about nothing. No-one is forced to buy such material, and the fact that people do shows that there is a market for it. There is no overwhelming evidence that pornography leads people into sexual crimes. The real danger is of a censorship which tries to restrict the freedom of people to watch what they want. The law and its application are purely subjective. Pornography is in the eye of the beholder. As long as children are protected, there is no reason to restrict adult access to sexually explicit material.

In contrast, many in society are deeply concerned about the portrayal of women. It is not just feminists who are fearful that women are presented merely as sexual objects often in settings of violence and submission. It can even seem that women really enjoy being raped. Such nonsense is in danger of masking the vulnerability of some women to being forced financially or in relationships to do what they would rather not do. It underplays the effect on the women who take part and on all of us who might see such material. The role of money-making in all this means there is always the danger of exploitation and the reducing of people to mere objects. Dirt for money's sake is still dirt.

The use of children and the rise in paedophile activities, particularly on the internet, reveals the danger of abuse and the corrupt activities that put at risk children and vulnerable adults.

Parents have difficulty in controlling children's access to computers and even television, video and magazine material. The watershed, explicit warnings on television and rating suggestions in cinemas and on television show that even producers recognize the need for children to be protected.

It is possible to distinguish artistic and literary merit in what we are presented with. This is not just a subjective judgment, for it takes into consideration the nature of the explicit material, its aim and the effects. Even if there is no proven link between watching pornography and committing sexual or violent crimes, it is hard to deny that all of us are affected by what we see and society itself also becomes gradually more tolerant of things that should not be tolerated. The world of virtual reality is opening the door to explicit sexual crimes, with apparently no consequences. We will need a morality which helps cope with that level of reality.

Christian perspectives

Christians share many of the concerns of the rest of society. The need to prevent the exploitation of women, children and the sexually vulnerable is crucial. We are all affected by what we watch, and society is in danger of accepting the unacceptable. Women and children should never be portrayed as sexual objects. They are not here for the titillation of men. It is also extremely difficult for parents to monitor their children's activities at all times. We need local and national controls over sexually explicit material and checks on access to videos, films, television and the internet. There are increasing numbers of computer control aids available.

The Old and New Testament encourage people to live morally upright lives (Leviticus 18 – 19; 1 Corinthians 6:9). The prohibitions on adultery, prostitution and unnatural sexual activities are part of the preservation of family life, which is a cornerstone of a healthy society (Deuteronomy 27:20–23). The Bible describes us as being engaged in a struggle between light and darkness, and we are always in danger of being conformed to the standards of the world around us (Romans 12:2). Paul recognizes that in Christ we do have freedom, but that our freedom is limited by whether something is beneficial or not (1 Corinthians 6:12, 19).

We are all affected by what we watch and are in danger of acting and copying what we see. The only way of safeguarding the vulnerable and ourselves is to avoid pornography and to seek governmental and local controls to restrict the availability of such material and access to it. More positively, we need to follow Paul's advice – 'whatever is true, whatever is noble, whatever is right, whatever is pure, whatever is lovely, whatever is admirable – if anything is excellent or praiseworthy – think about such things' (Philippians 4:8).

Something to think about

Why are people drawn to pornography?
How should we define what is pornographic and distinguish it from art and literature?
What are appropriate limits to freedom of expression and the freedom to watch?
How can we create positive images to help raise the artistic and social perceptions of all of us?

So what?

Each week my students come and read me an essay on some moral or ethical topic. They have read and studied the subject. They have presented a careful setting out of the context, a description of the issues and main views, a critique of these views and finally drawn their own conclusion. Then I ask them, 'So what?' They have spent a week of their lives thinking about an issue and responding to it, so what happens now?

In the same way, if you have read this book, it is only right and proper to ask, 'So what do we do now?' My hope is that the questions at the end of each section will help everyone see the complexity of moral issues and the need to think very carefully about how to respond to them. In particular, I hope that people will be asking, 'How do Christians actually make moral decisions?' If the introduction suggested that you were about to have a 'starter for ten', then this section points to how you can go much further.

Christians need to use some way of approaching moral issues, and the following approach tries to do justice to an overarching, biblically based way of looking at ethical questions. It deals with the nature of the action in question, the principles on which the issue rests, the motives at work, the people affected and the consequences of whatever is decided and done.

The nature of the action

What is done and not done is not neutral. Actions and omissions have very specific natures. They are something in themselves. It is vital that we ask what exactly is involved in doing this particular thing or refraining from doing it. Killing, lying, acting sexually, caring and nurturing are all descriptions of various actions, and we should be clear about what we are actually doing or refusing to do and why that is the case. The ability to justify what we do points to a clear understanding of actions and all that is involved in them.

The principles at stake

Behind every decision and action there are principles. Often they may conflict with each other, which can make the problem a moral issue and very difficult. We need to ask what principles are involved. For Christians, the Ten Commandments, the Sermon on the Mount and the teaching and commands of Jesus, Paul and the other Old and New Testament writers set out clearly the basic principles which are part and parcel of Christian belief and practice. Those who have no religious faith still work with principles in their moral decision-making. Many of these principles are either drawn from religion or are parallel to religious norms and precepts. There is wide common agreement about the importance of, and need for, fundamental principles in order to build unity and resolve disputes in morality.

The motives at work

Jesus taught that our attitudes and motives matter. They are as serious as our actions because they lead to what we do. If I slap the face of a student all of us would agree that that was not a nice thing to do. If I explain that I had noticed a rare bug on the student's cheek and that the bug was about to give a fatal bite to the student, then I had no alternative but to kill the bug. The best way of doing that was to slap the student's face. Now the same action is seen in a very different light. The motive transforms the morality of, and our attitude to, the action of the face slapping. Motives do matter, as we see from murder trials. The difference between manslaughter and murder is the criminal intent (the *mens rea*). If there is an evil motive, that makes the act more serious and worthy of greater condemnation. Likewise, good motives can change our attitude towards an attempted action which does not turn out quite the way intended. Motives count in our moral reflection on actions, even if it is sometimes hard to be clear about our own motives, never mind the motives of others. Usually, however, the motives are pretty obvious from the character and kind of person we are dealing with and their pattern of behaviour over a period of time.

The people affected

Morality exists between, and for the benefit of, people. What we do and what others do to us affect us all. When we are trying to assess the morality of a situation, action or person, then we need to consider who is involved and affected, in what ways and to what extent. People matter and what is done to them is important. Christians are deeply committed to the well-being and flourishing of all humanity. That means taking seriously the people involved and affected by actions and inaction and considering whether they are helped or harmed, benefited or damaged by what will happen or has been done.

The consequences

People often imagine that Christianity and other religions are only interested in moral principles. The more I read the Old and New Testaments, the more I see that God and Jesus Christ are deeply concerned about the results of what people think, say and do as well as what they fail to think, say and do. The consequences of our thoughts, words and actions do not affect just the here and now. They have an eternal significance. In the giving of the law, God warned that if we do not obey him and keep his commandments, then there will be serious consequences. In parallel, if we do keep the law and obey God's commands, then we will flourish. Jesus warned that how we live now affects our eternal destiny. Feeding the hungry, visiting those in prison, clothing the naked are all rewarded, but failure to do these kinds of loving actions means eternal separation from God. The consequences of what we do matters and needs to be assessed in reflecting on the morality of options, situations and people.

All of us have to answer for ourselves before the judgment throne of God. When we are called to give account of what we have done and why, then it is vital that we have previously considered what kind of answer we will give. While *Question time* does not pretend to give the answer to all the questions asked, it does offer one way of approaching the questions and issues we all face.

Further reading

Atkinson, D. and Field, D. (ed.), (1995), *The New Dictionary of Christian Ethics and Pastoral Theology*, Leicester: IVP.
This is an excellent starting point because it offers general introductions to the major themes and then traces the issues through their various forms. It also offers a biblical perspective on individual moral problems and concerns. Not least, it provides a helpful, balanced reading list for further study after each article.

Cook, D. (2001), *The Moral Maze*, London: SPCK.
This is a guide to how we do Christian ethics. It explores secular perspectives, different moral frameworks and offers a biblically based approach to moral decision-making. The method is applied to the two areas of abortion and euthanasia. The book is widely used in theological colleges and schools.

Cook, D. (2002), *Through the Moral Maze*, London: SPCK.
A different approach to the way that people actually make decisions and then an extended development of how to use the nature of actions, principles, motives, the people affected and consequences. This is then applied to fertility, genetics, sexuality, war and peace and environmental issues.

Hays, R. (1996), *The Moral Vision of the New Testament: Community, Cross, New Creation*, San Francisco: Harper.
A well-regarded approach to New Testament ethics using key categories to help apply and understand what the New Testament has to say on moral issues.

La Follette, H. (ed.), 2001, *Ethics in Practice*, Oxford: Blackwell.
This is a secular look at ethics in a little theory and wider practice. It balances different secular perspectives, so is not one-sided. It offers a wide variety of views dealing with different topics in different ways, but it does provide insight into how secular philosophies approach moral questions.